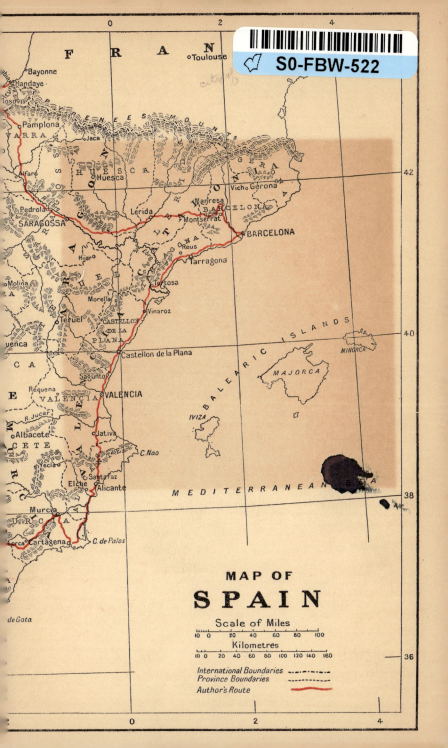

MAP OF
SPAIN

Scale of Miles

10 0   20   40   60   80   100

Kilometres

10 0 20 40 60 80 100 120 140 160

International Boundaries ·—·—·—·
Province Boundaries - - - - - - -
Author's Route

Spain in Silhouette

THE MACMILLAN COMPANY
NEW YORK · BOSTON · CHICAGO · DALLAS
ATLANTA · SAN FRANCISCO

MACMILLAN & CO., Limited
LONDON · BOMBAY · CALCUTTA
MELBOURNE

THE MACMILLAN CO. OF CANADA, Ltd.
TORONTO

GARDEN AND TOWER OF THE MEZQUITA, CORDOVA.

Spain in Silhouette

By TROWBRIDGE HALL

New York
THE MACMILLAN COMPANY
1923

Press of
J. J. Little & Ives Company
New York, U. S. A.

CONTENTS

ILLUSTRATIONS

Illustrations

Spain in Silhouette

Spain in Silhouette

1

In the Country of the Basque

September 25

Spain, the land of romance, of legend, of heroes! It is to be ours. We are on our way. We thrill even now to its magic. The glamour of the Alhambra by moonlight, the strange beauty of the mosque at Cordova, the actors of the Old World stage, Cervantes, Velásquez, Murillo, and those children of the brain, Don Juan, Don Quixote, and El Cid, the Campeador —all crowd their way into the glow of expectation. We hear the click of castanets as lithe-limbed Carmen, a red rose glowing in the midnight of her hair, sways in questioning pose before her Torero lover. Or perhaps we catch the soft twang of the guitar as a black-cloaked figure kneels beside the iron-grilled window of his inamorata. Thick and fast come memories of written enchantments. We are aflame with anticipation. *Hasta mañana!*

"Tomorrow" is here, and we are crossing the bridge over the river Bidassoa that separates the cities of French Hendaye and Spanish Irún. At the far end is the border custom house, its officials lazily lounging in voluptuous repose against the entrance door or sitting straddle-legged on chairs, smoking the eternal cigarette. Whatever the hour, by day or by night, indoors or out, in good weather or bad, alive—and possibly dead, the Spaniard and his cigarette are inseparable.

But the approach of "pretty woman" brings to their feet these lolling figures clad in brass-buttoned brown suits sashed with bright orange. They stand at attention, greeting us with a courteous sweep of their gay, rakish leather hats. Can these be the terrible Spanish customs officers? Shades of American "customs"! They actually apologize for presuming to turn over the contents of our portmanteaux. Perchance our trunks may be rifled in train transit, but if so, it will be very politely, and, after all, "vice and virtue are largely matters of opinion—and climate."

One traveler in Spain relates that while his bag was being most deferentially ransacked, a dutiable bottle, marked "Brandy," was brought to light. "What is this?" asked the customs officer. "I am not absolutely certain; it was given me," replied the traveler. "Then the only way to make sure is to try it," immediately responded the officer. A corkscrew was found, the bottle opened, and two glassfuls emptied. With an appreciative smack the officer rendered as his judgment that the bottle was correctly labeled, but added, "The package being broken, it is not dutiable."

Little need is there for a boundary line to mark entrance into Spain. The city of Irún, less than two hundred yards from France, possesses not one single feature in common with Hendaye. The very earth changes from *la terre* to *la tierra,* and the people have cloaked themselves with a haughty dignity never seen on the French side of the river. Even the houses take on a different form, their roofs jutting out beyond the walls, and balconies of iron projecting far into the streets. Over the railings of these aërial platforms shaded by black-striped, yellow awnings, the señoritas lean for hours, affording alluring pictures to the passers-by, at whom they gaze with so studied a disregard as to excite suspicion in my discerning companion. It takes a woman to catch a woman!

That unpronounceable name on the lamp-post at the street corner, *Ondarrabiko Karrake,* means, so we are told, the road to Ondarraba. Such was the ancient name of Fuenterrabía long before the Roman hordes overran the world. These conquering lords, not understanding the Basque tongue any better than we, rechristened the city "Fons Rapidus." This gradually transformed itself into the present-day name of Fuenterrabía. But the Basques are tenacious and cling to old names—witness, the lamp-post. No one can convert a race steadfastly insisting that they are the only descendants from Adam and claiming that the Basque language was spoken in the Garden of Eden.

High up on the bank of the sluggish Bidassoa the rich umber roofs and pale walls of the quaint old city are silhouetted against the sky. We turn towards it, following the road to Ondarraba through a medieval gateway blazoned with the proud title of *Muy Noble, Muy Leal,* and *Muy Valerosa,* finally climbing our way up the steep and narrow street from which the sun is almost excluded by overhanging roofs and jutting balconies. The street is so narrow that from these balconies heads must be bent far forward to get even a glimpse of what is passing below. Happening to look up, we catch sight of many inquisitive eyes peering between gayly fluttering hangings of multicolored rags—the entire population having exposed its night bedding of scarlet-striped coverlets and brilliant blankets on the balconies for the daily sun bath.

At the top of the hill, extending into the street, are the fortress-like walls of the Church of the Ascension—rather appropriately named, considering the stiff climb. We push open the doors of the vestibule inquiringly and seem to see cradled on the empty air two baby figures in fluffy long clothes—for the shadowy, black-draped phantoms who are holding the children are submerged in the semidarkness. At that moment from within the church comes a priest vested in surplice and stole. He carries two lighted candles, which he thrusts into the hands of the waiting women. The soft, flickering light aureoles the heads of these young mothers. Fondly clasping their tiny babes, they kneel before the priest, to be sprinkled with holy water and receive the blessing necessary for all Spanish mothers after childbirth before they

5

may reënter the church. Even so the mother of Christ, nearly two thousand years ago, carried her child to the temple and was purified.

A place for dreams is this ancient temple, and we allow our fancy to fill it with a picture of the past—a magnificent procession passing in stately grandeur into the building. Glorious music peals and thunders as the Bishop of Pamplona and all the clergy in sacerdotal robes approach the nave. The arrogant King of Spain, Philip IV, brilliant in silver-embroidered costume, enters first. He wears his picturesque broad-brimmed hat, fastened with a large diamond clasp to which is attached a pendent pearl that hangs far over one side. Behind the king is his daughter, the Infanta Maria Theresa, gorgeously attired in white. They make their haughty way over magnificent Persian carpets wrought of glittering threads, up to the gold-brocaded dais, high and theatrical, within the choir, where the priests in sumptuous vestments await them to celebrate the proxy marriage between Maria Theresa and Louis XIV of France. Today the sacristan proudly displays these very vestments, worn for the first and only time nearly three hundred years ago. Their beauty of color still untouched, they are the treasure of the church—and the envy of the connoisseur collector.

From the shadows of the church to the dazzling sunlight of the deserted-looking Plaza de Armas is but a step. Is it the sudden glare or astonishment that causes our eyes to blink as we read the sign on the massive façade of the building that takes up one whole side of the square:

THIS ROYAL PALACE AND CASTLE
OF THE EMPEROR CHARLES V
FOR SALE

A "castle in Spain," built not in the air, but actually on firm foundations laid, so they claim, in the early eleven hundreds, may now be ours for the proverbial "song." Is it its eighteen hundred and fifty bedrooms that deters our "singing"?

The view from the roof terrace amply repays the clamber up rickety stairs. One gains an uninterrupted vista of the far-stretching Pyrenees rising high into the sky, that seems to invest these beautiful mountains with a majestic serenity. They make a superb background of violet, sharply defining the white houses of the village

7.

of Pasajes, tiny houses crowded around an inland sea that resembles an Alpine lake, as it nestles within the encircling arms of the hills.

It was from Pasajes that Lafayette took ship for America in 1776. Immediately in front of where we are standing the English legions under the great Duke of Wellington crossed the river to victory, passing, as did the Israelites of old the Red Sea, when a wind storm drove back the tide and laid bare the water-bed for an hour or two.

With the crystal of imagination we repeople the little island—Ile de la Conférence—lying amidstream. Small as it is, it has played a real part in the annals of history. Louis XI and Louis the Grand, Francis I and Henry IV, the great cardinals Mazarin and Richelieu, Isabella and Maria Theresa, each has occupied this tiny stage. The treacherous tides are slowly gnawing its life away, but this ancient donjon will stand for many more centuries like an advance sentinel, jealously guarding the frontier of romantic story.

September 27

What necromancy has been at work over night! A hundred years has been bridged while

journeying the few miles that separate Fuenterrabía from San Sebastián. Dirtily picturesque
Fuenterrabía, with grass-grown streets and half-
ruined houses, lives on the glories of the great
past—Spain's most treasured possession; while
San Sebastián is so new and clean as to be almost
un-Spanish.

When Madrid is sweltering under a blister-
ing sun, this city of natural charm plays the rôle
of summertime Spain, the pleasure ground of
royalty. In the troubled days following the
death of her husband, Maria Cristina, the
Queen Mother, courageously broke through
rigid court etiquette, abandoned the traditional
summering cities, and came to this lovely
Basque country, searching health for her baby
son and peace for herself. Perforce, nobles and
courtiers followed, and San Sebastián, one of
the most beautiful watering places in Europe,
became also one of the most fashionable.

In a simple English-like cottage, overbur-
dened with the high-sounding title of *Palacio
Real,* Alfonso XIII grew to manhood, spending
his days in the great outdoors, acquiring a taste
for sports and a love for San Sebastián that will
never leave him. Summer after summer he
gayly exchanges the splendor of a palace for the

homely delights of little Miramar hidden within a grove of trees and overlooking the beautiful waters of La Concha Bay. Alfonso, known as the most democratic king in Europe,—and practically, not theoretically, democratic,—more than lives up to his reputation. Perchance his shrewd ears have caught the sinister remark of one of his subjects, that if he would not be democratic, he would not be king. It is characteristic that even the intimate connection that has grown up between this watering place and royalty has not deprived it of the least trace of old Basque democracy.

Today the streets are placarded with posters announcing the "finals" between the most celebrated pelota players in all the Basque land. How much this means one can guess from the fact that in Basque life the pelota court holds second place only to the church. Few villages are too poor not to possess some sort of court,—though any bare wall will do, with the result that sometimes churches have had to raise pathetic petitions for enthusiastic youth to desist practicing against their walls—at least during the celebration of mass.

We were fortunate in being able to get box seats for the game, and more fortunate still in having them close to the royal enclosure—royal in name only, for, except in its more central position, it differed not a whit from ours. At the time we arrived, the building was already jammed with a shrieking mob, making a bedlam unintelligible except to the initiated.

Here was a long rectangle, three sides solid walls of masonry, the fourth formed by steeply banked rows of spectators over whose heads, on a protruding balcony, were the boxes. At play were six men, three on a side, using a very small and very hard ball. To start the game, one player drops the ball to the floor, and on its rebound catches it in the *cesta,* a kind of hollow wicker hand strapped to the forearm of each player. The *cesta* might, perhaps, be described as an elongated scoop, like the bill of a flamingo. With incredible swiftness the ball is hurled against the front wall, from which, with a sound audible all over the court, it shoots back, sometimes as far as the back wall, two hundred feet away, rebounding to the center, to be caught by one of the opposing team and returned to the front wall. So the ball is kept in play until a fault is made by one side or the other. The six willowy figures, dressed in white, with soft silken sashes of the color that christens them with the official name—Blues and Reds—slip about like cats, their steely muscles ·sending the ball in such rapid flight that the eye follows with difficulty. The betting odds change with almost every passage of the pelota ball. Crowds of bookmakers, wearing the scarlet cap of their profession, swarm among the spectators, wildly shouting for recognition and stopping only to throw to some signaling customer a hollow rubber sphere enclosing betting slips. The din is indescribable. Those who are backing the winner yell jubilantly; the losers howl even more deafeningly, attempting to attract the bookmaker's attention and possibly recoup their loss.

Our interest shifts from the game to the royal box, although there is nothing to mark royalty —no decorations, no guards, no lackeys, just the King and Queen, the Queen Mother and a friend. They attract no special attention and are given none. As we look, the King is leaning far over the box's edge, watching this favorite game with evident enjoyment. His rather sober face becomes extremely animated, and his fine eyes change expression with every change of play. Now and then, at a signal, some book-maker flings him a rubber betting ball, which he will catch adroitly, fill with money, and send flying back. Her Majesty, the Queen,—*"Muy Reina,"* they call her,—sits back, off to one side. She is a trifle impatient, possibly, at the noise about her, and yet her manner is charming. Her reputed beauty, unlike that of most beautiful women, exceeds its reputation. Clean-cut features, the fairest of fair skins, softly waving light-brown hair, and a pleasing smile make Queen Victoria one of the really beautiful women of the world. The game finishes in a final uproar, and the royal party slip out unattended.

Almost next door to the pelota court are the race course, the bicycle track, and the Plaza de Toros. As a general rule, only *novilladas* are given at this plaza—fights between small bulls of little spirit and matadors who are far from proficient. The bulls in *novilladas* have great woolen balls covering the tips of their horns, so as to render them comparatively harmless; while the matador conceals his inexperience by masquerading in eccentric costume. The day we were present, he was dressed to represent Charlie Chaplin, and instead of the regulation sword, he carried the Chaplin bamboo cane with which he would repeatedly jab at the disgusted bull, who would promptly respond by knocking him down, both the man and the bull disappearing in a cloud of dust. Up would jump the man, perhaps to pull the bull's tail or leap up on his back, capering around the ring in all sorts of idiotic antics. Now and then he would permit himself to be buttocked, flying through the air, to land sprawling on all fours. He played the clown until the crowd tired and called for the bull's death. Then a real sword was brought, and this buffoon bungled the poor beast into heavenly pastures. Little blood was shed—except the bull's. It is a sort of opera comique for the childish-minded and for tourists, who imagine they have seen a real bullfight. Of course the *novilladas* is despised by bullfight "fans," or *aficionados* as they are termed, yet the plaza is always crowded, and every Sunday human torrents pour out of the building, losing themselves in the streams of the city's lower life.

October 1

This morning we walk along the sea walls, through the Paseos de Zurriola and Salamanca, where so often the ocean snarls and grabs at the stony barriers with claws of white, spitting an angry spume far over the top. Today, however, the water is like liquid green, hardly moving under the faint breeze, while the serrated mass of the Pyrenees behind a sun-sparkling haze looks like a vapor of amethyst.

It is Sunday, and we must first visit *Buen Pastor,* the Church of the Good Shepherd. No, we need not get up early or disturb the even tenor of our lazy way. The indulgent priests have made churchgoing comfortable, as well as comforting, for the fashionable world. With mass at quarter-past twelve, one can sleep late and still salve his conscience. About the entrance door lounge perfumed dandies unabashedly eyeing the señoras and señoritas as they enter the church, and awaiting their exit before commencing to saunter along the Avenida de la Libertad. There they will pass and repass the same elderly women, always dressed in black and always stout, who will be sure to have in tow some seemingly demure maiden, whose velvety eyes are rarely indifferent.

In the late afternoon there will be a throng on the Alameda, that broad boulevard of shaded walk flanked by two streets, separating the new city from the old and replacing the ancient city walls. All the world will be there, the several social streams placidly flowing side by side, but each seldom overflowing its own bank. It is a popular saying that on the Alameda are *salón, comedor,* and *cocina*—parlor, dining room, and kitchen. Here and there groups linger, some to watch the passing show, some to listen to the music. Only for a moment does the real wealth of fashion pause, then moves on to the Casino— one of the best known in Spain. Here, as members or casual visitors, the *aristocracia* promenade up and down the terrace, to see and to be seen and to listen to the famous orchestra. Touched with Basque democracy, this orchestra plays for all the world to hear, although it is led by the musical aristocrat, Señor Arbos, royalty's favorite conductor.

Congregated in the park below, which still bears its old-time Arabian name, *Alderdieder* (most beautiful place), are the "plain folk" listeners, some moving slowly, yet chattering and gesticulating with a vivacity granted only the Latin race; others sitting on benches, between palm trees, listlessly smoking cigarettes; all taking their ease, and content that their neighbors do the like.

Plainly noticeable are the many tall, strapping girls in their stiffly starched white caps and long gold earrings, and the big-bosomed women garbed in red cloth petticoats and velvet bodices, with bright-colored handkerchiefs as headdress. These are the famous Santander nursemaids in national costume.

But it takes a woman's eyes to see the jaunty soldier boys swaggering about, always in pairs and always flirting with the same girl, as though bound by union rule to an equal distribution of labor. I have often wondered if these same observing eyes saw the two women with carnation cheeks who just then laughed an invitation to me, without taking the least account of her presence.

But it is Queen Nature who has blessed San Sebastián with her greatest charms. The storm waves that hurl themselves against the outside rocky shore never penetrate into the exquisite blue shell of San Sebastián bay, except in gentle billows that come as though "hungering for calm," gently rolling up the magnificent beach to break into silvery foam. This lovely La Concha Bay is almost locked in the embrace of curving hills, with Montes Urgull and Igueldo standing guard at the extremities—the same Monte Urgull that can tell such glorious tales of the gallant Englishmen who died for Spain, and who now, in their last sleep, lie in a place of

17.

great beauty in the side of the cliff washed by the sea.

From the raised terrace of the Casino we are looking out upon a magical sweep of celestial blue. In the growing dusk—the overpowering spell of Massenet's "Cid" upon us—we easily surrender to the witchery of night's "thousand eyes," responding to the sensuous thrill of the music and the gentle murmur of the waves, as in accompaniment they pulse and purr on the beach below. When at last darkness falls, there is left with us imperishably the magic of the hour and the fascination of the city.

October 8
While waiting

Truly, it should have been a Spaniard who conceived that pompous phrase, "Let every man be master of his time," for no one in this sophisticated world knows so well how to hold time in leash, treating it like a poor relation and keeping it ever in the background. To every demand your Spaniard always replies with a cheerful *"mañana,"* seemingly never supposing it possible to do today what can as easily be done tomorrow or, far better, several remote morrows after the morrow. No wonder the proverb says,

18

"Let my death come from Spain, for then it will be long in coming."

Here we are with the automobile all loaded and waiting at the door, and our passports not yet locally viséed. A good week ago we called at the *Ayuntamiento,* dubious as to whether the government could find sufficient blank space on our already much-decorated papers of citizenship to stamp its permission for travel; but, with many courteous bows and much courtly politeness, we were assured that it was possible. Call *"mañana,"* they said. Eight *mañanas* have come and gone, and the passports still lie on the pile of forgetfulness. What are we to do? "Try the power of gold," someone whispers, and, behold! gold speedily sets the governmental machinery agoing. We have thereby learned our first lesson in that system of bribery that, like an ugly sore, runs its festering way through most of the lower grades of bureaucracy—exceedingly small salaries being the excuse for taking advantage of official life.

Evening of the same day

Driving along the base of these Pyrenees of Alpine height, it is easy to understand Voltaire's description of the Basques as a fearless people

19

who dance on the summit of mountains. Scattered over the high slopes of vineyard-clad hills or clinging desperately to the inhospitable sides of barren rocks are the homes of this courageous race that came into Spain some fifteen years before the birth of Christ. Of inherent democratic stock, they fled to the mountain tops for protection, determined at all costs to keep their independence. A most interesting people, these Basques. They speak a tongue few men can learn. Tradition claims that the good God, wishing to punish the devil for tempting Eve, banished him to the Basque country with the command that he should remain there until he had mastered the language. But at the end of seven years God relented, finding the punishment too hard. The tale is implicitly believed by the peasantry.

Indeed, all Basque traditions, even those which have their origin in superstition, are not to be doubted, for are they not stamped with churchly approval? And the influence of church and religion is all powerful even today. In the daily life of the Basque there is not an act, however unimportant, that is not prefaced by some sort of homage to God. The first mouthful of a new fruit, the first slice cut from a loaf of bread, passing a church or meeting a funeral, even the knife stroke which kills an animal for food, invariably brings a sign of the cross or a prayer.

The old spirit still turns the eyes of the Basques toward back ages, and they stubbornly lead the same life their fathers led before them. If we but had the devil talent of the Hebrew mythical Asmodeus and, like him, with magic power could lift the roofs of houses, we should see, as the clock tower sounds the morning Angelus, these stern old farmers sleepily pulling on their long velveteen trousers and hurriedly slipping down the stairway. Each one stops before the roughly hewn basin placed near the doorway a century or more before, when the house was built. The front edge of the bowl is smoothly polished by the thousand rough fingers that have rubbed it as they touched the holy water. The peasant blesses himself with the sign of the cross and immediately starts his daily prayers, continuing even as he works—so as not to lose time. Following closely after him and observing the same rites, comes the mistress of the house, who takes possession of the deepest and most shaded spot in some near-by brook where "as the stars begin to dim before the morning's rays," she spreads out her big basket of linen in preparation for the morning attack. With a few rough stones she dams off as best she can a little pond, into which is thrown the gayly colored wash. She is joined by other house-wives, and soon in minor key is heard the rhythm of pounded linen to the *forte* accompaniment of a ceaseless chatter of gossiping tongues. Towards eleven o'clock the Angelus sounds again, this time thirty-three strokes in commemoration of the thirty-three years of our Saviour. Then all work is stopped, the men remove their scarlet caps, and the women bend their heads—in un-conscious pose for the magical brush of another Millet.

2

Pamplona, Saragossa, and Montserrat

Pamplona, the capital of Navarre, is our luncheon stop. A trivial enough incident to chronicle about the city that Pompey rebuilt,— and some say honored with his name,—when there are so many notes of interest about Pamplona. It is here that the ever famous Ignatius, born to the purple in the near-by castle of Loyola, forsook his passion for glory,—and also, incidentally, for a rich widow,—turned ascetic, and became a "soldier of Christ." Elsewhere this phrase may have become only a religious symbol, but here in Spain, in the company of Jesuits, the order Ignatius founded, Christ's army is a living reality.

Pamplona claims, too, for her own that rare violinist, Pablo de Sarasate. Merely to mention him is to recall the great mass of raven hair always tumbling in disorder about his pale face as he gave his distinguished rendition of the Mendelssohn concerto or perhaps the "Jota Arragonesa," when his wild, dark eyes would gleam with fervor and excitement, for he loved best of all this national hymn.

And you who dote on medieval romance, would find here in the cathedral chapel of Santa Cruz the tent chains that railed in the Moorish encampment at the picturesque battle of Los Navas de Tolosa. The very sight of these brings to the ear attuned to fanciful history the cries of Allah, the bugle blare of the Christian warriors, the shock of armor, the murmur of chants, the fantasy of heroic ages long past.

But we are seeking the real Spain of today, and luncheon in the Fonda de la Perla discloses a national psychology that is the outgrowth of purely modern conditions. In earlier ages the Spaniard always entrusted labor to slaves, the word "labor" sounding to him like an insult; but today, with work a necessity, he salves his pride with novel regulations. The waiters of this little *fonda* scornfully refuse all proffered tips, but when the luncheon bill is paid, ten per cent of the total is added as their honorarium. Still, in this country, if one is *simpático,* one is sure to be well treated.

Peculiar to the Navarrese landscape are the huge circular masses of rock topped with black, gloomy castles like sentinel watch towers. And curiously enough, in this kingdom of many real castles, "Fata Morgana" is constantly revealing chimerical others among the weather-beaten cliffs—lofty pinnacles that require no vivid imagination to turn them into real feudal towers lording it over the phantasmal stone houses and bristling along the perpendicular sides like a porcupine pursued. "Morgana" must have laughed as, in the ages past, she raised these mighty wraiths oftentimes to the confusion of the enemy of this buffer kingdom. Indeed, in early days the province was always on the defensive, for when the warriors of old had nothing else to do, they would kill time by invading Navarre.

Sunburned, dusty plains, stony, trackless wastes, Navarre; yet crowded with romance! How well do we know our Cervantes? Here at Pedrola was the magnificent palace of the "Duke of Villahermoza," who "invited the Knight of the Sorrowful Countenance to visit him, offering the welcome justly due so great a personage." Later Don Quixote bowed himself from out this castle, taking his way, as we, toward Saragossa, arriving in a day or two at the river Ebro, "whose sight was very delightsome." Alongside the bank was moored the enchanted boat into which he ventured, hoping to carry aid to another knight in distress.

But if these splendid adventures are blurred by time, will not Castellar bring "Il Trovatore" to mind? It is on the heights just above us, deep within those lovely woods, the fortress to which Verdi led Leonore to follow the troubadour Manrico in complete surrender, relinquishing all wordly things for love.

Just before the walls and spires of Saragossa appear, the valley broadens, and evening's tempering light touches the dreary plain with softening fingers. Beyond the distant figures of peasants returning home from work, driving their flocks before them, the sun sets in a glory of purple and rose, splashing Nature's canvas with a splendid background.

October 12

Have you ever heard the religious myth of the Apostle Saint James? In his wanderings about Spain, he found himself one evening with his disciples on the bank of the river Ebro, under the walls of Cæsar Augustus—Sara Gusta—Saragossa—and while kneeling there in prayer, the Virgin, seated upon a pillar of jasper, appeared before him. Throwing himself upon his

face, the Apostle tremblingly awaited the fore-
ordained message. Soon, from out the holy
enveloping mists, came a voice commanding
him to build on that very spot a chapel for the
worship of the Virgin, and giving assurance
that for all future time Saragossa would be distinguished by unprecedented devotion. The
blessed Virgin further promised that the pillar
upon which she sat would remain to the end of
the world as tangible evidence of her coming.

A skeptic one may be, and yet there can be no
humoring smile at a belief that has wielded so
powerful an influence over all succeeding generations. In that glorious defense of the city
against Napoleon, when so great was the slaugh-
ter that the living were unable to bury the dead,
the "Pilar Madonna" was the mighty bulwark.
This was the fearful battle when even priests
fought, dropping their swords only to admin-
ister the consolation of religion. And not only
priests, but women were in the fray, led by the
"Maid of Saragossa." This heroine of Byron
fame, battling side by side with her lover,
snatched the howitzer match from his drooping hands as he fell mortally wounded and,
shedding "no ill-timed tear," manned the battery in his stead. During all those hellish days,

27

when the smoke of gunpowder kept the city in a continual twilight, there were daily processions of the "Pilar Virgin." To her the emaciated, hungered peasantry would kneel, praying for courage, and under the stimulus of religious fervor they found the bravery that carried them to death on the fast-crumbling ramparts.

The people of Saragossa have preserved their old-time fanaticism, and even in this generation there is not a hut in all the Arragon region in which there does not hang an image of the "Pilar Madonna." Scarcely a man or woman is there whose neck is not encircled by a cord carrying her metal semblance, not a lip to which *"Virgen mia del Pilar"* does not immediately come in every joy and sorrow.

Today the Pilar cathedral is crowded with a fervent multitude. Within a circle of beautiful marble columns, surmounted by a canopy of velvet sprinkled with golden stars, is the holy of holies. On her pillar of jasper stands the revered image, nearly invisible under a magnificent tunic heavily hung with jewels that flash back the lights from innumerable candles. Never did a royal courtesan in the mad luxury of the Golden Age possess such pearls as Saragossa's passionate piety has loaded upon this Virgin!

PILAR CATHEDRAL, SARAGOSSA.

THE MONASTERY OF MONTSERRAT

The mosaic floor of the sanctuary is packed to suffocation with kneeling worshipers, and far outside, from wherever the sacred image can be seen, kneel other votaries, their heads touching the pavement in adoration. More thousands keep pouring in through every door of the church, reverently tiptoeing their way into the presence of the divine one. They are taking the places of those who, after paying their first devotion, in unbroken procession slowly file by the opening in the massive wall at the back of the shrine where appear a few square inches of the jasper pillar. Ragpickers and ladies of wealth, peasant and peer, old and young, hale and infirm, all press closely upon the heels of one another, each kneeling, as this small opening is reached, to kiss yet deeper the hole scooped into a smooth hollow by centuries of other pious kisses.

We find our way from out this superstitious gloom into the sunlit plaza, noisy with a band of carnival merrymakers. Never before have we seen more grotesque, more ridiculous paper heads than these worn by *"los gigantes"*—giant heads atop pigmy bodies—gathered here to dance before the cathedral. The streets are nearly impassable. There are maskers on foot and maskers in carriages—the carriages hung with colored paper ribbon, binding the wheels and half strangling the occupants. Trailing behind are bands of young men and girls in serpentine line, singing gayly. But never a song of intoxication mars the picture; there is no lapse into unbridled familiarity, only now and then the occasional touch of some playful hand inviting us to join their revelry.

At length we are seated on the balcony outside the hotel window overlooking the broad Calle del Coso, always the carnival center. Even during the black days of the French siege of 1808, with the city maddened by sorrow, October 12, as today, saw the same sort of rollicking crowd. Only at the funeral bells of Torre Nueva, telling that an enemy gun was about to be fired, did the dancing stop. At that moment the conscience-stricken throng would kneel, to tell their rosaries during the deafening roar of the cannon, rising again, once the sounds ceased, to resume their mad dance of folly.

Today the calle is like a beehive in swarm; there is constant coming and going, in and out, here and there, everywhere. High dignitaries of the army in gala attire strut their way across the plaza; whining beggars ply their trade;

elderly women artfully conceal age under graceful mantillas; young girls cling to sweethearts,
oblivious of all the world; romping, laughing
children run in and out among the throng.
There are gay country folk, picturesque in their
blue and black *mantas,* garments that only par-
tially conceal an evident imprint of poverty, and
yet, loosely thrown about the shoulders, like
Roman togas, serve to accentuate the haughty
bearing natural to poor Arragon. (Isn't it
evident, the source of our English "arrogant"?)

At times there will be a momentary lull, and
a few lazy ones, in indolent pose, will lounge
against the corners for support and idly watch
an obliging friend preparing to strum his guitar.
No sooner does the musical sound reach the ear
than some young girl will click her castanets,
and all is movement again. In an instant there
is an ever-widening circle of joined hands, with
dancing and singing to the accompaniment of
hand clapping and foot stamping. Then the
balconies become alive with spectators, and even
the cheery bronzed old woman on the corner
just beneath forsakes her chestnuts simmering
over the charcoal fire—to the joy of thieving
urchins who have scented the delicious odor
from afar.

But suddenly all frivolity stops short. Black-cloaked figures are gliding silently among the merrymakers, pointing to the nearing candle glow reflected in the sky. A word suffices, and the center of the street is swept clear, leaving orderly rows on either side. There is a hushed silence as the procession approaches to the beat of muffled drums—mournful and portentous. The light from a thousand candles strikes the walls, bringing into sharp relief the balconies filled with devout onlookers, and softly illumining the eager faces on the street below. In the lead are heavily embroidered silken banners hung with supporting cords, each in the eager clutch of some grave-eyed little girl. Torrents of the faithful stream after, holding aloft lighted candles and chanting their naïve melody of the Litany of the Blessed Virgin. Such singing is never heard except where religious faith is equally firm. Robed in gorgeous vestments and surrounded by attendant acolytes, all in scarlet, like embryo cardinals, the church dignitaries come into view. Then even the sound of drums ceases, and all is still—save the cathedral chimes. Another moment—and with one voice the vast throng cry out, *"Alli viene Nuestra Señora."* They fall on their knees, and the

32

Pilar Madonna in a blaze of glory is carried by on the shoulders of stooping penitents. Paganism, not Christian religion, you say. But are not "pagan and human almost synonymous"?

As the solemn sound of reverent footsteps loses itself in the darkness, loud laughter can be heard at every corner. The ceremony is over, and life is too brief to be further shortened by mournful thoughts. With the rest of this contrast-loving people, we at once forsake the memories of soft, flickering candles and plaintive melody for the cafés bright with the blatant glare of electric light and the still more blatant music of jazzy orchestras. Here we take our first sip of Spain's insidious *aguardiente,* which has a sharp burning taste, rather disagreeable. Someone says that perseverence with this, as with other human affairs, has its reward, and soon there will develop a liking which time will increase to enthusiasm. By way of confession, it must be admitted, that under the potent influence of this liquid magic, the shining lights of the plaza shone even more brightly, and the eyes of the passing señoritas seemed more than ever provocative.

To borrow another traveler's happy phraseology, this city rejoices in the questionable pleas-

ure of possessing two cathedrals, which, like a
man having two wives, brought nothing but
bickering and jealousy until another Solomon
hit upon the happy idea of conferring the same
dignity on both, cutting the year in two and
making each cathedral in turn, for six months
at a time, the official See of the Bishop.

It would be difficult to find a greater contrast
to gaudy, painted, theatrical Pilar with her
Byzantine domes and minarets than that offered
by La Seo's spacious, restful grandeur. On suddenly entering this cathedral from the open
sunny square, there is the impression of having
been plunged into a fathomless sea of darkness.
But the eyes gradually become accustomed to
that dimness so conducive to prayer, and Seo
proves more of a place for worship than a rendezvous for sight-seers. There is an atmosphere of dignity in its broad aisles lined by huge
columns that reach up to the murky twilight of
the lofty roof; a venerable air that brings every
separate part of the cathedral into harmony,
possibly through long association and being
habituated for centuries one to the other. Of
course Seo must have her shrine too, and a tab-
ernacle of black and white twisted pillars marks
the spot where the Virgin once spoke to some

kneeling priest. But he, poor man, not having been left any tangible proof by the momentarily forgetful Virgin, was charged with jealous conspiracy by the cathedral of Pilar and failed of sainthood for future generations to worship.

But one can never overhear the real secrets of a city by haunting dim cathedrals, so once more we make our way into some of those tortuous, ill-paved streets that even yet have not entirely recovered from the carnival of hell through which they passed when Saragossa "spat in the face of Napoleon." From here we cross over the seven-arched, fifteenth-century bridge spanning the Ebro, where, against a darkening sky, we can take our fill of the cathedral's sensuous silhouette. Here we may print a last mental picture of the grim old city, whose street sounds, mingling together in a sort of musical refrain, drift up to us long after the view itself has disappeared and the far-away foothills have wrapped themselves in their night mantle of deep blue-gray.

October 15

Dreary as had been the latter part of our road to Saragossa, with its lonely houses clinging to barren rocks of ashen gray, it paled before the

35

frightful desolation of the country beyond. A semi-African, waterless, treeless desert of waste sand, wrinkled by parching winds, with only an occasional oasis village hardly distinguishable in color from the ground on which it stands, it is so filthily dirty that it must breed death even more quickly than it can give birth to living souls. It is a country of arid, formless shape like that which imaginative physical geography gives the earth's surface in prehistoric times. An atmosphere of somber, melancholic bigotry makes quite understandable the belief that it is the casting of an evil eye that causes death and illness among the flocks and the families of the little village through which we are passing. It is a Hades of a road,—not even paved with good intentions,—and the country about lacks even the little water and good society necessary to distinguish it from Lucifer's abode.

But there are compensations in the many appealing pictures. Here comes a group of peasants, bundled in rough, brilliantly striped cloaks, their heads bound in gaudy bandannas, their chins drawn within colored woolen scarfs, wearily scuffling behind the donkeys upon which their women sit sideways, ahead of heavily laden baskets. Again and again we plow through such droves of mischievous burros. Long-suffering, hard-working, clever beasts they are; some stepping carelessly, like fatalists resigned to the blows probably in store for them; others proudly appreciating that the peasantry cannot do without them. As a matter of fact, in most of the passing carts the drivers are not driving, but, stretched out at full length in heavy sleep, they are trusting to the faithful donkey to show more intelligence than his master.

At Manresa we linger just long enough to visit the *Santa Cueva*—the sainted cave around which are now built the protecting walls of a convent. Here Loyola, the first general of the Jesuits—"the best organized and most famous army that has ever fought in the war for Christ" —lived in seclusion for several years. Passing the greater part of each day and night upon his knees in an agony of spirit, he strove to purge himself of sin so as to be better able to guide the troubled souls of others. Loyola had come down from Montserrat, where, like a knight of old, he had performed the vigil of the armor. Hanging up his sword in relinquishment of secular warfare, he watched till dawn before the altar, waiting for a benediction upon his new career in soldiering.

37

Wondrous Montserrat! The sacred mountain first shows herself to us curtained by a filmy cloud. This ghostly apparition in gray, "crowned with a fantastic diadem of tortured stone," rises suddenly from out the great plain of Catalonia, far into the skies. A sudden rift in the nebulous blanket reveals a group of giant mountains, each, with mighty arms aloft, holding the profane at bay; for this spectral row of rocky pinnacles was, according to legend, guardian of the Holy Grail, that precious reliquary carried from Jerusalem to the sanctuary of Monsalvat, to be confided to the care of a band of holy knights. These are the knights made famous by the genius of Wagner. At the time of the Crucifixion, when "there was darkness over all the earth and the veil of the temple was rent in twain," this gray mountain mass is said to have shuddered with sympathetic horror and, in agony of spirit, to have torn itself asunder, opening a wide and rugged ravine that split its way from the sacred settlement to the utmost top. No more terrifying spot could have been selected for the safe-keeping of the present-day Holy Grail.

Long years ago some poor shepherds, herding their flocks on the lower slopes, perceived a strange light appearing and disappearing among the rocks above. As, mystified, they gazed upon the uncanny sight, strains of music floated down to them, unearthly in their softness, luring the shepherds to climb the mountain side. Guided by a subtle and fragrant odor, they chanced upon a brightly illumined grotto in which reclined the miraculous image of the Virgin brought to Spain by Saint Peter. On reporting their find, the clergy in solemn procession carried this wonderful being from out her long resting place toward the plains below. But after traveling a short distance, the Virgin refused to move farther, and the priests were forced to erect an altar where they stood. This spot was a wondrous shrine of Nature's making long before pygmy man did his best to spoil it.

We make our pilgrimage through the portal of the monastery, one of the oldest and most celebrated in Spain, into the courtyard, where the yellow-brown cloisters open their saint-named doors to the faithful, who, year in and year out, toil up this steep incline to make their offerings to *La Santa Imagen*. The visitors' rooms in "Saint Gertrude" are veritable convent cells, with walls of rough plaster, one small, iron bed, a jug of water, a wooden crucifix, and now and

39

then a broken bit of mirror—probably in con-
cession to worldly feminine vanity. Certainly
Saint Gertrude is endowed with less beauty than
virtue! But how immaterial the material, when
we are once outside amid the overwhelming
grandeur of these lofty peaks that seem to smite
the anguished heavens! Up and up their gray-
green sides cling white marble statues, stations
of the cross, telling the story of Christ's ascent
to Calvary. God has surely marked this place
with his own imprint—a strange and troubling
beauty.

The cathedral bells are ringing out their call
to *Las Oraciones,* and soon the angel's saluta-
tion to the Virgin, "Hail, thou art highly
favored, the Lord is with thee!" will be chanted
to the people in sonorous Latin. We enter. The
temple is filled with a thick haze of incense.
From the dome a shaft of light finds its way to
the shrine, balconied high over the chancel, covering it with a purple glow. There stands the
Black Virgin of Montserrat arrayed in cloth of
gold, a crown of emeralds upon her forehead
and glittering diamonds around her neck. Over
the bent heads of those kneeling to her in adoration float the solemn measures of the *Salve,* sung
magnificently by the school of religious music.

This school is taught by the few remaining monks, and once heard, is never forgotten. As the last note floats away, there is a scurry of feet through the nave to a stairway behind the altar. One and all mount the spiral approach to the Black Virgin, kiss her, and leave the church. We linger for a moment in the little room whose walls are covered with rude ex-votos so absurd as to incline to laughter. But the touching simplicity of these humble offerings grips the heart, and more likely than not, instead of the anticipated laugh, there will come a sympathetic smile.

When the shadows are creeping up the mountain side, we take our way toward Barcelona. The peaks above glow as though tipped with burnished gold, and over the far-away sea spreads a crimson flush, promise of the morrow's glorious dawn.

3

Catalonia, Land of Contrasts

In a country whose national ideal of happiness is to do nothing, Barcelona would seem to be out of place. From way afar we heard the labored breath of the great city moving and working in mighty travail, and upon reaching the dingy outskirts we could see nothing save miles of ugly factories whose soaring chimneys belched forth clouds of smoke. But the real Barcelona—Cervantes called it the flower of the beautiful cities of the world—is not even sooted by the grime of business; for the sons of toil are confined to distant outskirts, and the unsightly buildings are carefully hidden in the far background.

Primitive Barcelona sprawled on the shores of the Mediterranean with her feet in the water; then, like some monster from its depths, she stretched out her long, grasping tentacles and seized the far outlying villages to feed, with their labor, her hungry maw. The result? Thousands upon thousands of toilers have embraced the faith of anarchism and have accepted its tenets as gospel, thereby making Barcelona one of the most turbulent cities in Europe, the gathering place of lawless socialists and fanatical bomb throwers.

It scarcely needed the revolution of ten years ago to reveal public discontent. That was indeed a fierce demonstration of the wrath of a long-suffering people seemingly without means of redress. In wild despair they set in motion evil forces that soon got beyond control. Streets were barricaded, railway lines were uprooted, telegraph wires torn down, churches sacked and burned, priests hunted through the streets to be murdered before their very altars. Even the gentle nuns were driven back into burning convents by the stones of the infuriated mob. These last-named depredations, it must be understood, were directed not against the church, for the Catalonians are a religious people, but against the priesthood. As in the days of the French Commune, the women were even more ferocious than the men.

The inevitable end came with wholesale arrests, and in the cells of that grim fortress on the high hill overlooking the sea were witnessed the brutal cruelties of medieval

43

times. Quivering flesh was burned with red-hot irons, bared bodies were brutally beaten, finger nails were ruthlessly torn from their sockets, all in an attempt to force confession. The climax in this hideous drama was reached when Ferrer, who dearly loved the people and had devoted his life and fortune to private education, was shot, blindfolded, as the light broke over the sea, suffering the martyrdom of a dreamer and enthusiast. "Incredible; it can't be true!" we exclaim. And yet today we stand on the top of Montjuich, in the shadow of the fortress whose dominating guns keep the claws of anarchy well clipped.

It is one of those quiet, peaceful autumn mornings, when on the far horizon a perfect azure sky melts into an even more perfect blue sea. Long time we stand on the mountain, gazing at the beautiful Mediterranean that stretches out like a vast sheet of clean blue paper touched, miles and miles away, by the brown mark of the Balearic Islands, the only spots on a canvas otherwise clean except for the busy harbor in the near foreground.

This coffin-shaped mountain is aptly named "Montjuich," Mountain of the Jews, by reason of the Jewish Cemetery on the slopes toward the city. Few Jews, they say, can "live" in Barcelona, for the Catalonians out-Jew the Israelites in shrewdness and trading.

A Catholic cemetery is on the farther side of Montjuich. It is traversed by long, deserted streets flanked by straight walls of equal height, all honeycombed for those who prefer such burial to resting in the bosom of Mother Earth. In these holes, in rows like books in a library, lie the inhabitants of this silent city; some with orifices tightly sealed; others faced with glass, leaving just enough space for a picture, a curl of hair, or a baby toy. Gaudy-looking hearses are forever unloading their grim burdens. One in love with Life and loath to look upon Death instinctively turns away; but most of the coffins have a front of glass, and it is impossible not to see within. On a bed of tinseled flowers lies a lovely boy, his tiny head haloed with fair, curly hair. One less ornate holds an aged figure, the seamed face powdered and rouged, the hair crimped and oiled, the feet encased in shoes of screaming newness; and the shoes, always new, are invariably removed before burial and sold —to him who cares not if he wears "dead man's shoes."

45

But let us away from death and disaster to the gay Rambla, the center of life and animation, that avenue of arching plane trees that enclose a broad walk, with carriage roads on either side. It stretches its green, flowery way over a small stream that once meandered through the middle of the city from Tibidabo to the sea; hence its Arabic name, Rambla—"dry river bed." Some would-be wit calls it "Rumbler," from the perpetual roll of vehicles, for street cars are forever clanging by, while slow-moving donkey carts and horse-drawn carriages alternate with speeding automobiles. A ceaseless, changing procession of vehicles there is, with "all Barcelona" afoot on the promenade. There are itinerant merchants crying their wares, and porters and chimney sweeps silently bidding for trade with the red cap and the sooty brush of their professions. Comely shop girls stroll arm in arm during the luncheon hours, with ogling youngsters —and probably an envious "ancient"—slyly spying from afar. And ample-bosomed mamas, with eyes ever alert behind fast-moving fans, anxiously watch their slips of daughters.

To us—as to all—feverish hands tender bits of dirty paper—*"quien quiere la suerte"*—lucky lottery tickets, sure to win. Bird tenders and

RAMBLA DE LAS FLORES, BARCELONA.

TEMPLO DE LA SAGRADA FAMILIA, THE MODERN CATHEDRAL
OF BARCELONA.

flower sellers salute us with their vivid wares; for this paradoxical city has given the busiest part of its bustling thoroughfare to a flower and bird market. Under the planetas lining the Rambla de las Flores are rows of stalls blooming with flowers of orange, lilac, and blue, over-topped by the feminine pink cheeks and laughing, confident eyes of their owners, who are perched on high stools. From other booths on the adjoining Rambla de Estudios come the inviting songs of yellow canaries, bidding us buy. Everyone wears flowers or carries flowers; everyone comes here to see or to be seen; and the ever-changing crowd personifies the very soul of gayety.

At length we have reached the Mediterranean and the end of the Rambla. Don't turn back; walk with us farther, along the palm-shaded Paseo de Colón, bordering the sea. There you will find the statue of the immortal Columbus sharply etched against the sky. High over the sea it rises. On a tall pedestal stands the glorious dreamer, pointing to the far-away lands of his discovery.

It was in 1493 that Barcelona welcomed Columbus back from the New World. From every window and every balcony hung costly brocades, tapestries, embroidered shawls, and oriental carpets. Amid the joyous acclaim of the multitude that crowded the streets, he quietly rode his way, followed by gentle West Indians and native carriers, bearing the brilliant plumage of unknown birds, skins of strange animals, marvelous plants, and still more precious metals. These were his thank offerings to Ferdinand and Isabella. The waiting King and Queen, seated in the open square under a canopy of brocaded gold, rose as Columbus approached, and received this man of genius as brother royal. Then, in a burst of exaltation, the vast multitude fell upon their knees and began to intone the *Te Deum* of gratitude. Such is the picture history gives us.

But revolutionary Barcelona gives us another film, taken only a comparatively few years ago, when the news of the loss of Cuba appeared upon the city billboards. With one accord, as though some finger had touched an electric button communicating with every brain, the reading mob rushed to the Paseo de Colón, collecting, as they went, cobblestones, old eggs, and decayed vegetables. These they hurled at the statue of this prophetic Genoese, in violent reproach for having dared to find so troublesome a

48

new world for Spain. Modern aggressiveness does not mix well with ancient sentiment.

October 18

We were awakened early this morning—that is, early for Spain—by tinkling bells just outside the window. Going to the sunlit balcony, we saw on the pavement below a herd of snow-white nanny goats waiting to furnish milk on order. Their herdsman was a picturesque rascal, decked out in short, black-velvet breeches. On his feet were hempen sandals, with black ribbons crossing the instep; around his waist, a gayly colored sash; and tied about his head, a silken kerchief. There he stood at the very entrance of the aristocratic Ritz, blocking the way of an approaching Rolls-Royce, hoping that someone from within might perchance wish his goat's milk for the morning's breakfast. Oh, land of wondrous contrasts! Imagine such a scene in front of the Ritz in Paris, New York, or London! But in democratic Spain even Señor Ritz is powerless.

For some of Barcelona's treasures one must search well. Here, as elsewhere in Spain, many of the best architectural bits are in remote corners. Only after many winding turns

49

through narrow, angular streets crisscrossing one another do we find the beautiful cathedral, hidden away from the noisy world of modern traffic. Tattered old crones are sleepily crouching within its shadowy entrance. Awakened to speech by our approach, their raucous voices whine in unison, *"Limosna por amor de Dios,"* and the well-coached babes-in-arms stretch out expectant hands. Without response we hurry by, to be pursued by maledictions as far as the fountained cloisters. Here the glare of midday becomes "filtered sunlight," and eternal peace is usually found.

To our surprise the solemn silence is broken by the strident cry of geese. According to fabled story, during the great siege of years ago all Barcelona, weary of fighting, slept in the seeming security of a stormy night. But under cover of this cloaking darkness the enemy crept almost within striking distance of their unsuspecting foe, unheard save by some strutting geese that hissed so loudly they awakened the city to the threatened danger. Since that time geese have been honored by a home in the cloisters of the cathedral. Indeed, the Patio fountain, its water falling in regular cadence and, like some narcotic, carrying the mind into the harbor of sleep, is known as *Fuente de las Ocas*.

Somewhat later there is another unexpected sound. Precisely at noon comes the piercing note of a big bell struck sharply by a greased and bewigged sacristan in scarlet robe. Even before the noise dies away, the pitter-patter of innumerable small feet is heard, and, scampering in from every side, come sleek and fat cats— thirty of them—fifty—sometimes a hundred—to feed and then contentedly stroll back to more exciting haunts, reappearing only at the ringing of the bell the following day. The story is that some eccentric—a woman, of course—left a huge sum to the cathedral, carrying the strange proviso that all stray cats of Barcelona should be fed once a day, and, honoring this bequest, the cathedral clergy have taught the cats to come at the sound of the dinner bell.

If one may properly term the cloisters solemn, the church can certainly be called austere—typically Catalonian, they say. Just as her women dote on somber tragedies, so they love dark, gloomy cathedrals, appealing to the national pessimism. From out the shadows rises the choir, which Spanish custom places in the cen-

51

ter, like putting one church bodily within another. Over the choir, as we enter, the smoke of service incense hangs suspended, and to the sobs of cellos can be heard the chant of men choristers. Around and around the walls of the outer church walk sunken-shouldered, pale-faced priests, the almost extinguished fire of their barren lives flaming only in black, piercing eyes. With heads bent low over breviaries, their emotionless lips keep mumbling the offices of the day. Immediately beneath the high altar lies the crypt, and before its gated entrance we see shadowy groups of women kneeling in half obscurity, their black mantillas, like bits of cloud, so dimming the picture that the blurred light shows only Madonna-like faces with wide-open, pathetically seeking eyes, striving to penetrate the mysteries of God.

Down the stairway, amid lamps forever burning, sleeps the patroness of the city, Santa Eulalia, her body as beautiful and perfect today as when she fell into her last sleep, hundreds of years ago. An imprudent and skeptical bishop once ventured to prove this truth, but as he unwound the last cloth with which her body was swathed, he was struck deaf and dumb and could never tell of the wondrous sight beheld.

Would that I had the power to picture for you the tormenting character of this Catalonian Gothic with its thousand exquisite details, a severe coldness that calms the bodily passions, and with it all a warmth that nourishes the longings of the soul. Wait with us until the afternoon sun, when the superb stained windows, among the finest in Spain, will blaze gloriously, one after the other, changing the interior into a vast symphony of color, and inspiring within us the wordless prayer with which centuries of praise and worship have charged this holy atmosphere.

How very different is the inconceivably modern cathedral, the Sagrada Familia (Sacred Family). This dream of an idealist is slowly being visualized in the *Ensanche,* the new quarter of Barcelona. The architect, Señor Gaudi, believes architecture is capable of telling a story, and in solid stone he is trying to relate the tremendous romance of the world's creation. Struggling for realism, he has copied from life-plaster-casts each one of the million figures massed upon the towering spires. The fragile butterfly as well as the gigantic gargoyles glowering from above, and even the saintly men and women, all are taken from actual life, painstakingly conceived and laboriously created. Some think Señor Gaudi mad—a price too often paid by men with new visions; but most of Barcelona acclaims him as the wonder of the architectural world.

An interesting if somewhat exasperating development in the design of houses has shown itself in recent years. The city has been bitten by the modern love of display, and garish houses look out at us from every street; houses which material success has overloaded with a strange ornamentation born of the unhappy marriage of Teutonic and French *Art Nouveau*. On the Paseo de Gracia, the fashionable walk of aristocracy, always filled with a rapidly moving crowd and whirling automobiles, there will be pointed out an eccentric building erected as the sequel to a passionate love affair. A well-known señorita promised to give herself to her lover only when he should build a house in which he could mount to her room by automobile. Here stands this strange monstrosity—now quite a prosaic apartment house—with a circular driveway leading up to what was her room and his expected Paradise.

But neither material success, enslavement to business, socialism, nor anarchism has been able

54

ARCHITECTURE TYPICAL OF ART NOUVEAU IN
NORTHERN SPAIN

NEIGHBORHOOD LACE-MAKING IN THE STREET, BARCELONA.

to kill the artist soul of Catalonia. In Barcelona, early each May, are held poetic jousts or floral games, for competition in verse. Here newly written poems are read for the first time to an attentive gathering of literati, ecclesiastics, and workingmen,—for, unbelievable though it may sound, certain poetry is as well known among the laboring class as among the intellectuals. All that the proud winner receives is an artificial flower and the title *"Maestre en Gay Saber,"* an honor as keenly sought today as by the famous troubadours in the fourteenth century. Poets are so many as to be innumerable, though perhaps the best known is Verdaguer, whose "Atlantida" is claimed to be one of the finest poems of Catalonia. In painting, Barcelona has also mothered many a celebrity; there is, for example, Fortuny, that great "magician of jeweled tone."

Despite the fact that all of Spain is musical, Barcelona's fame in this realm is not less than in the other arts. And it is not alone the master musician who is a connoisseur. The idle lounger at the little wicker table of some Rambla café, staring between sips of chocolate at someone else's wife or daughter, is likely to call upon the café orchestra for some "trifle" from Grieg—"a

55

sea of charm into which the weary soul may dive to rise again refreshed." Someone writes that only in Catalonia can literature be held to flourish or art claim sincerity or science boast a following. Strange people these, loving work and loving play, and playing as hard as they work.

On one of those days when, as Burns says, "It's hardly in a body's power to keep frae being sour," we climb to the beauties of Tibidabo, letting Nature play upon the strings of our better selves. How beautiful it is you can perhaps imagine when I tell you that Tibidabo (I give to thee) is the mountain selected by the devil from which to show our Lord all the wonders of the kingdom of the earth. Fiercely disputing its slopes are hundreds of *torres* (country houses) surrounded by splendid groves of figs and pomegranates, with terraces and gardens gay with flowers. These are interspersed by great clumps of palms, whose feathery tops wave slowly in the light breeze, like fans fluttering in the fingers of green-veiled señoras. Far below at our feet, in undisguised revelation, as though secure in her youth and beauty, lies the mistress of the Mediterranean, while in the far-back distance stretches a maze of encircling mountains, over which at sunset trembles a line of faint fire whose color can be mixed only on the palette of God.

Why, O brilliant city of contradictions, holding first rank in business, distinguished above others in literature, music, and art, must you forever play the discontented child of Spain! We leave you with a heart full of warm and grateful feelings and with the words of Cervantes upon our lips: "Fare thee well, Barcelona, the home of courtesy, the refuge of strangers, farewell!"

October 20

We are saying *adios* to the practical North, which has little time to waste on midnight serenades or soft whisperings behind alluring *rejas*. We have turned toward the soft, voluptuous South, where, under moonlit palms and shadowy tangled vines, they sing songs of love without thought of the morrow.

Our way is close beside the Mediterranean, through flowering orchards and vineyards of luxuriant grapes—the very vineyards that Pliny must have described. The sea is brilliantly, startlingly blue, flecked with little boats, whose tricornered sails, like the wings of sea gulls,

skim before the fresh autumn breeze, a breeze
that pushes the restless waters far up the rocky
shore, spraying us with its silvery foam. This
quite rivals that famous drive over the lovely
Corniche in the Riviera. It lacks only the snowy
Alps. The hills here are olive covered, Bib-
lically pastoral, were it not for the castles sen-
tineling the hilltops. These last, incidentally,
in their newness and brightness are very unlike
the proverbial castles of romantic Spain.

But abruptly all is changed. The very stone
walls surrounding the fields of yellow stubble
take on a look of age. Crumbling ruins show in
the distance. Then a magnificent triumphal
arch bestrides our road. We rumble through it,
getting back the echoes of long ago. We hear
the tramp of the legions of Augustus as, with
eagles aloft, they marched through this very
Portal de Bará on their triumphant way to
Tarragona.

Last night I stood by the window of my little
room in the Fonda de Europa, looking out
toward the "Balcony of the Mediterranean" and
watching the storm clouds that had been gathering all day. At last, ready for battle, they came
swooping down upon the city, spreading a bar-
rage of lightning flashes that turned the wind-

tossed waves into a sea of fire. In another second all was shrouded in darkness. The houses opposite were blotted out of sight. The broad Rambla de San Juan, just below, disappeared, and at length the entire town, wrapped in an inky pall, faded from view. Behold, the very moment for which I had long been waiting was at hand. I might now indulge in my favorite diversion of leaving the present for the past. Upon the storm-effaced present-day Tarragona it would be easy to build from written memories that mighty Spanish city of Julius Cæsar, numbering more than two million people, which, years before Christ, stood on this very spot.

My waking dream brings the quiet of dawn. Nothing is to be heard save the occasional tramp of the soldier guard or the stumbling footsteps of some rioters sneaking home from stolen pleasures. Through the warm morning air come spicy odors, wind-wafted from the shrubs covering the roofs of the patrician dwellings. High above all can plainly be seen the palace of Emperor Augustus. The vestibule door is ajar, showing inner walls overlaid with costly marbles and inlaid with amber, ivory, and mother-of-pearl. Over the main entrance crouches a satiny-black magpie ready to reëcho for every visitor the obsequious welcome offered by the *"salve"* drawn ·in mosaic on the threshold below.

As day breaks, the streets fill with a motley throng. Many are rushing to secure early places in the amphitheater. They impatiently push their way through the narrow thoroughfare already choked by loitering fakers selling wonder-working nostrums and by interpreters of dreams and venders of amulets, each waiting to waylay the pious and afflicted as they bring offerings to the temple. From time to time the people draw aside to make way for some slave-manned litter. Or they pause to stare at the painted women whose figures, draped in almost transparent snow-white tunics, can be more than guessed, despite the amethyst-colored *palios* thrown about them; their hair fastened by jeweled nets is entwined with chaplets of roses, and curiously wrought golden bands encircle the neck and bracelet the arms. Once they have passed, the soft-sandaled mob laughingly close in behind, shuffling and padding their way toward the amphitheater.

For hours these plebeians pour into the arena's seven entrances, until, not only every seat is filled, but every opening from which a view can possibly be had, and the building is jammed with a great expanse of expectant faces, all aflush with excitement. The ceremonial procession soon begins to wind about the oval. Guards bearing waxen tapers lead the way for barbarian prisoners, who follow sullenly, knowing well the fate in store for them—a fate kept graphically in mind by a long string of trailing wagons piled high with coffins. The sight of these doomed men seems to stir up the worst passions of the populace, and their screams of delight, mingled with the roar of captive beasts, now beginning from their subterranean cages to scent their human prey, makes an uproar that grows louder and louder, like a series of storm waves against a rocky shore. Here and there between the seats run canals filled with water, cooling the air. At regular intervals throughout the amphitheater stand vessels for the burning of Arabian perfumes, to smother the smell of blood. The sun, by now high in the heavens, filters through the purple awnings, filling the great space with a bloody glow as if foreshadowing the awful scenes to follow.

At the sound of trumpets there enter blindfolded gladiators—burly ruffians in complete armor and slender, naked fighters equipped only with spears. Pushed towards one another, some blindly clutch in deadly embrace, body interlocking body, until they are fairly torn limb from limb; others wildly brandish swords and spears trying to find the way into shrinking flesh. The crowd, intoxicated with death, roars its approval, and, as if in answer to the shouts, hundreds of wild beasts are let loose among the survivors. Come tigers from far-away Asia, panthers from Africa, ferocious bears, and cunning hyenas, all purposely famished to make them more eager for the feast. They are followed by javelin men, who fling their winged darts into the struggling mass, leaving not a single thing living.

Next there appears a host of convicts sentenced to death, each carrying a crucifix upon his shoulder. As they near the center, they are seized by slaves who stretch them on the cross, nailing their hands and feet to the wood. Then, raised aloft, they are fastened to the ground, to remain until the miserable men droop to their last agony. With their death, the hearts of the rabble rest content.

By this time the hour of Saturnalian revelry has arrived. Hundreds congregate at the baths to listen to some poet or philosopher, who carries his precious papyrus encased within a bronze tube. Amid the splash of swimmers or the sudden plunge of divers, trial of some newly written poem or recently evolved Stoic maxim will be complacently made. The more crowded the bath, the greater the attraction. The vast hall swarms with nude men and women—the very dregs of society and the very cream of aristocratic froth.

Splendid marble columns support the roof of the swimming room; the spaces between are walled perhaps five feet high, and then to the roof they are filled in with magnificent lattices of heavy, cast bronze. Into the pool, from enormous lion heads of silver, flows water clear as crystal in which is reflected the painted blue ceiling, dotted with stars. Everywhere are a prodigal magnificence and a ministering to sybaritic tastes such as can be duplicated only in Rome. Precious marbles covered with even more precious stones are lavishly displayed, while such extravagant fancies as burning cedar wood sprinkled with ambergris is used to keep the bathers warm when at rest; or perhaps fountains spray them with the perfume of violets as their bodies are being anointed with Arabian oils. These disciples of Epicurus invert the order of nature, rioting all night until another dawn calls them to sleep.

Such was my reverie, and such was the actual city in the year 26 B.C.

The next morning, while lingering on the lovely terrace, so happily called the "Balcony of the Mediterranean," gazing out upon the now unruffled silvery waters, whose mirrored surface impudently denies either storm or cloud, I somewhat hesitatingly confessed to "D" the sleepless dream of the night before.

Why is it, do you suppose, that women fanatically cling to the ridiculous theory that all manly emotion, or lack of it, is traceable to his digestive organs? To my outpouring came the somewhat disconcerting assertion, "I am not at all surprised after what you ate last night." And come to think of it, that was an astounding dinner. On arrival at the Europa I had delivered myself of some very carefully studied Spanish phrases, but the proprietor showed a strange unfamiliarity with his own language and only at the word *pescado,* when I was expressing my liking for fish, did a gleam of understanding appear in his intelligent eyes. That one word, *pescado,* must have burned into his brain,

consuming every other single thought. The
dinner was an orgy of fish. We began with
tiny, long-tailed shrimps, rosy red, and a bowl
brimming full of gaping mussels. Next came a
speckled trout, to be followed by boiled eels,
their slippery, mucous coats still glistening in
the heated water. Then a spiny lobster appeared
upon the table, a baked fish, and a fish salad.
Not a vegetable, not a meat. And the proprietor all the while close to the table side, hyp-
notically "fishing" for compliments, his *"¿Le
gusta a usted? ¿Le gusta a usted?"* accompany-
ing our every mouthful.

Of course arguments never convince a woman.
She always insists upon her inalienable rights to
the last and conclusive word; so, without comment upon the truths actually lying at the bottom of my fanciful dream, I took my skeptic by
the hand and led her along the short Paseo de
Santa Clara to the upper city, where today still
stands the palace of Emperor Augustus, first
used by him in the year 26 B.C. I was even able
to point out the traditional spot where Cæsar
Augustus ordered promulgated his famous edict
described by Saint Luke: "Now it came to pass
in those days, there went out a decree from
Cæsar Augustus that all the world should be

enrolled. And all went to enroll themselves, every one to his own city. And Joseph also went up from Galilee into Judea to the City of David, which is called Bethlehem." A short step from the palace, we looked down upon the wave-washed ruins of the horrible amphitheater in which died, crucified, many of the early Christian martyrs.

Then we paid a flying visit to the Roman aqueduct, leaving the city by the Puerta del Rosario and winding along the Campo Santo, where drooping cypresses guard the dead—thrust into wall niches, one above the other, like bottles into the pigeonholes of a wine cellar.

Some two miles beyond, in a rough, deep ravine, amid a tangle of fanlike palmettos and wild thyme, stands the two-thousand-year-old water bridge, arching its way from hill to hill across the valley, defying Father Time to do his worst. A marvel to all, this titanic structure is a veritable miracle to the ignorant peasantry. They call it "Devil's Bridge," whispering, one to the other, the story of how in the dark ages Satan wooed a lovely Tarragonian maiden. Spurning his mere love advances, she was finally tempted by a promise of great wealth and worldly position to listen to his boasts of miraculous power. "Prove to me your omnipotence; build for me in one night a bridge across the ravine that runs through the Campo de Tarragona, and I yield to you." With the night came fearsome storms. The ground was rent apart, and from out the bowels of the earth sprang millions of shadowy forms that toiled and labored through the hours of darkness until morning revealed a hundred-foot-high bridge spanning the valley. But the maiden was seen no more, though on other wild, stormy nights the winds carry to the villages below the wail of some lost soul, followed by the awful sound of exultant chuckling.

Returning, we wandered about the prehistoric Cyclopean walls that encircle the city for more than two miles, making it, in early days, impregnable to every assault. The immensity of the foundation stones can be compared only with those of the Pyramids of Egypt. The stones remain, but the Titans who piled them are lost in the haze of mythological shadows.

Tired, but still determined, I told "D" that if she cared, and was willing, there were many' more remains of temples, a circus, a bath, and a theater that spoke with an old-time eloquence unsurpassed by any other Roman city in all

Spain. But she, tired too, pretended to be convinced and asked to see something modern. So we took our way to the only really new thing in Tarragona worth seeing, the cathedral, and that was begun in the year 1120.

On the summit of the old city the Mother Church has taken up her abode, lovingly watching from the heights her spiritual flock as it gathers about her on the slopes below. Though dedicated to God, it was built with a guardian eye seeking the physical safety of his children. This has given the cathedral somewhat the character of a fortress—a sturdy old building, very appropriate to its surroundings of antiquity. Its severe simplicity, however, is somewhat broken by the decorations of the main façade. About the doorway are grouped wondrously carved canopied niches for twenty-one statues of the Prophets, all supposed to have been in place at the beginning of the fifteenth century. Five of these statues are now missing. According to popular tradition they agreed between themselves to slip away, one by one, each hundred years—even saintly men, it seems, tire of too strict religious seclusion.

But once within the portal, frivolous thoughts disappear. The strange "luminous gloom"

68

characteristic of so many Spanish churches
brings a feeling of great solemnity. Unsuspected
emotions are stirred, and the soul recognizes the
house of God. With time the eyes grow accustomed to the shadowy light, permitting even the
untutored to revel in this almost unique, though
oftentime fantastic, collection of Spanish sculpture chiseled in early Christian days. On the
very sacred retablo hang many a spider and butterfly, wrought with all the minutia of a Japanese artist, while on the capitals of the columns
the imagination of the Romanesque stonecutters
has been allowed to run riot, alternating Biblical
scenes with beast fables. God is depicted drawing a tiny Eve out of Adam, and the Three
Wise Men of the East are economically placed
in one bed, restlessly awaiting the call of the
angel who is to guide them on their journey to
Bethlehem. Adjoining are a group of trembling
mice exultantly burying their old enemy, the
cat, who, however, having only counterfeited
death, suddenly springs from out the hearse,
chasing away the now terrified undertakers.

A long time we wander in the lovely cathedral
cloisters, where the sunshine gently pierces the
delicate carving of the columns which enclose

the patio, painting upon the inner walls, with golden brush, the tracery of other exquisite arches. The song of birds and the hum of insects fills the air, and from the choir comes the sound of solemn chanting, bringing a note of sadness, such as only Spanish music can, but with it, also, the promise of everlasting peace.

4

Valencia, Land of Plenty

Many days have passed since last I wrote. Not only is Titian autumn left behind, but winter has held us in his cold embrace until, weary, he has laid down his overheavy burden, which "the boy of a new year" with all the conceit of foolish youth has confidently shouldered. But I take pattern from one of Spain's famous teachers, who without warning was snatched away from his university classroom and kept in prison for five years by the pitiless hand of the Holy Inquisition. The very morning following his release found him back at his old post, beginning his regular lecture with, *"Decíamos ayer——"* (As we were saying yesterday——).

Today—as "yesterday"—the sea lies in flat calm, smooth as a mirror, but unreflecting, as if its mirror-backing were badly dulled. And in truth, the sky, which is the quicksilver lining for the mirror-sea, is a lowering black. But why should we wonder that the heavens are sometimes somber, at other times gay? Does not

Life's shuttle inevitably weave, for all alike, mingled threads of joy and sorrow?

The white hand of dark December still clings to mountain top even though March has summoned flowers and blossoms in profusion, scattering them lavishly along the foothills. But before we meet them, we must pass through the Campo de Tarragona with its thousands of olive trees raising their dusty gray heads. These low hills are tormentingly barren, for while doomed to eternal thirst, they are forever within sight of a tantalizing stretch of blue water. Patched with big yellow pieces of scorched earth, they are like the mantles of the poor. Here and there is a tiny plot of tilled ground that resembles a green handkerchief laid out to dry on the arid stone.

But within the delta of the river Ebro, which has torn its way from out the mountain fastnesses, is a luxuriant plain. Countless canals furrow the surface in a network of veins and arteries bled by *norias* (water wheels) that lift the life-giving fluid over sloping banks on to the hungry soil. In the center lies Tortosa, the haunt of pirates when the country was under the Moors. Once they lost this key to the fertilizing Ebro, the dark-skinned race never regained it, but were beaten back time and time again by the savage courage of the Amazons of early days. These warriors, incidentally, were rewarded for their heroism by the permission, dear to feminine heart, to import in perpetuity all finery free of any duty. Thanks to this favoritism, which is still in force, their fortunate children's children are today decked out in enviable attire.

A wayside cross marks the entrance into the province of Valencia and the birthplace (Castellón de la Plana) of one of her most famous sons, the artist Ribalta. In wise books we read that he was the first Spaniard to break the stiff bonds of medieval painting and adopt the freer style of the Italians. This was due, without doubt, to his long sojourn in Italy, and although these books neglect to explain how Ribalta happened to leave his own land and go to Italy, Valencian gossip is not so reticent.

Ribalta, so goes the story, worked as a laborer on his father's farm, going directly from there into a Valencian studio. Here he studied and painted industriously until the black eyes of his master's daughter proved more alluring than canvas virgins. Discovered one day making compromising love to her, he was dismissed in disgrace and sent to Italy. He spent several years there, until the longing to see his mistress became too strong for resistance, and he returned to Valencia.

It was late afternoon when, agitatedly, he knocked at the studio door, hoping to find his master out for a daily stroll, as was his custom. Even better fortune awaited him, his old teacher was away for the night. But as Ribalta ardently embraced his inamorata, his eye caught sight of one of those over-elaborated church retablos resting on a near-by easel. The teaching of his years in Italy rebelled, and, seizing a brush, he painted till sunrise, transforming a lifeless Madonna into a veritable masterpiece. At the very moment he was putting the finishing touch to this celebrated picture, the door opened and in walked the master. At once he recognized the genius of Ribalta's work, welcomed the truant, and all was forgiven. In almost ascetic solitude Ribalta spent the remainder of his life painting sacred pictures, never putting brush to canvas without first being shriven by some priest. "How slight a chance may raise or sink a soul!"

Late afternoon mists are hovering over Sagunto. It might well be the smoke of the famous siege that has made the city (ancient

Saguntum) immortal. Imagination touched by history paints the picture of the legions of Hannibal hammering with ponderous battering-rams at the city gates, the air filled with missiles of blazing pitch. Wall after wall crumbles. The desperate people seeing their last defense fall, in despair build a huge bonfire of all the wealth of the city, and as the scorching flames shoot heavenward, they throw themselves upon the pyre—a true holocaust. Not a man, woman, or child is left to meet the conquering Cartagenian.

But we do not linger in Sagunto. From afar can be seen the blue-tiled towers of Valencia. Soon we shall have reached the city of the Cid.

Later, the same day

El Cid, the Campeador,—Lord and Conqueror,—immediately after his triumphal entry into the city of Valencia, ascended its highest tower "that he might survey the earthly paradise he had won." Like him, we too mount the same long incline of El Miguelete.

Far below are Valencia's somber, mysterious streets, twisting and turning in puzzling direction, like so many open trenches. They are banked with low, flat-roofed houses overtowered

75

by oriental domes and sheathed in dazzling colored tile. Over the harbor of El Grao a few silvery clouds are lazily drifting, while outside the city walls is spread the fair huerta unveiling all her beauties under the splendor of a dying sun. As our eyes sweep the vast and splendid plain that stretches from the distant castle hill of Sagunto to the far-away mountains of Alicante, we seem to hear the voice of that ancient Moor who, at the approach of the Cid, had likewise climbed this very tower, for one last look at his beloved city. Gazing about him, his eyes filled with tears, and he cried aloud, "O Valencia, Valencia, trouble has come upon thee, and thou art in the hour of death!" In agony of spirit his trembling hands beat his breast, and over his long white beard the tears of sorrow fell, one by one. Small wonder is it that Rodrigo Diaz proudly wrote his wife, "Come and see what a garden is here. You may enjoy its beauties and revel in its delights, for I, the Cid, have made myself its mighty lord and master."

Tonight the long, narrow calles are aswarm. The entire city must be out of doors, and everyone is rollicking and gay as though the unquenchable spirit of eternal youth had taken

76

complete possession. With difficulty we make our way, halted at every step by street venders who squirm and wriggle among the slow-moving crowd, adding to the noise and confusion their strident cries of *"¡Carmelos, el rico coco, palillos, palillos!"* The beribboned packages of toothpicks thrust pleadingly into our faces are reminders that even tardy Spain's dinner hour must almost be at hand, and with the thought, nine o'clock sounds from the tower of Santa Catalina.

We are soon seated before a huge bowl of *paila,*—Valencia's favorite dish,—a concoction of beans, peas, and onions, small bits of beef, lamb, chicken, mussels, and shrimps, all covered with a highly seasoned sauce of dried tomatoes. It can scarcely be said that this compound belongs to the "poetical school of gastronomy," and time alone will disclose whether "nightmares" are among its ingredients.

March 16

Morning finds us at the entrance of the quaint Calle de Zaragoza, a crooked street, dwarfed into a winding lane by lofty El Miguelete, the cathedral tower that seems to block the further end. But we go farther today, seeking the other

77

entrance to the cathedral, La Puerta de los Apóstoles, where meets the Tribunal of Waters. The plaza in front is already beginning to fill with peasants from the huerta, their bronzed faces bright and fresh as though washed by the cleansing winds. Some are gathered in gesticulating groups; others are idly seated on the fountain steps, content that the sun shines for them as well as for the more favored. All are patiently awaiting the time when a bewigged sacristan, with the assistance of workmen in smocks, will erect a railing at one side of the doorway of the twelve Apostles. This is accomplished slowly, very slowly—for what is one day when there are so many in each year! At length, within the protecting iron, and just beneath the accusing figures of Saint Peter and Saint Paul, are placed eight plush chairs, each bearing in gilt the name of the irrigating district over which its occupant has complete charge.

A bailiff, rigid and unsmiling, takes his stand at the entrance gate, a brass staff, with scythe top, his badge of office. "Let the Tribunal begin!" he announces, and the eight judges, dressed in black smocks, black caps, and black *mantas,* solemnly take their seats. These eight men, elected by their fellow farmers, are absolute masters of all the water that feeds the vast huerta. Their decisions admit of no appeal. In their hands rests the fate of the crops, doomed to death unless by their order revived with a transfusion of this life-giving fluid. And the responsibility of men who know their decisions must be fulfilled shows on these sober faces.

The gathered people flock to the railing, pressing close against it, lest they miss some faltering word. The honk of automobile, the clang of *tranvías,* all the tumult of modern life swells and surges about the plaza. But the little court, as though wafted beyond the reach of sound by the heavily incensed air puffing from out the adjoining door, is all unheeding.

The complainants approach, one by one. Neighbor denounces neighbor. A few questions are asked. The judges in impressive whispers confer one with the other and, amid a hushed silence, announce their decision. There is no mystifying writing, nothing to confuse the ignorant, the punishment or acquittal is immediate. It is simple, honest, patriarchal justice, the same as given in the far-off days of the Moors in the same place, on the same day; the same as will be rendered by this *Tribunal de Aguas* as long as Spain is Spain.

If it happens that you have ever had the curiosity to read the *Chronicles of the Cid,* you will perhaps remember that it was at the Moorish Alcázar, the present *Lonja de la Seda* (Silk Exchange), that the Cid lived, with his wife Ximena. One day, while he was idly seated there in his ivory chair, messengers brought news that a vast company of Arabs was assembled in the plain about the city gates; Africa's great Emir had come to reconquer beautiful Valencia. Immediately the Cid and his wife hurried up the Alcázar tower and looked out over the plain toward the sea. "Behold, the green earth had turned white, so many were the tents! From afar came the raucous notes of tambours beaten by dervishes in wild frenzy, and Ximena was afraid. But the Cid comforted her, promising that before many days those same tambours should be laid at her feet and sounded in her honor. And so it came to pass."

This *Lonja de la Seda* is an exquisite bit of early architecture, despite the somewhat ornate carving decorating the main façade. There appear here, repeated many times, Valencia's coat of arms—those famous four bars brought into existence, so says legend, by Valencia's conqueror. Swearing to wrest this country from the hands of the Moors, he placed a blood-stained hand in vow over his heart, leaving on his white tunic the parallel marks of four fingers.

Circling about many of the windows are pudgy little angels, half buried in stony clouds, as though seeking to escape the loathsome gar-goyles protruding from under the battlemented roof. So unspeakable are these gargoyles that visualize the erotic filth of some depraved mind, as to leave us shamefaced even after entering the glorious star-strewn vaulted hall. The ceil-ing of this hall is upheld by splendid spiral pillars. Around the upper wall, for all the world to read, runs a Latin inscription prom-ising the merchant who neither cheats nor takes usurious interest that he will inherit eternal life—but gossip claims that few merchants read Latin.

Through the open doorway float confused murmurs from the Plaza del Mercado—the city market place. A few moments later, in its midst, we are hustled and jostled by a busy hive of shoppers, disputing and bargaining with the tired women huddled behind back-breaking baskets heaped with vegetables, which they brought to market at the shivering break of day.

Amid this whirlwind of gay petticoats and multicolored shawls, the blind are tap-tapping their way, certain of sympathy from the poor, and as for the rich, "Comfort cannot too frequently be reminded of life's misery." Over there a blind trio in tow, as always, of some barefooted, ragged boy, halts on the sidewalk. Filtering through the crowd we hear a thin-voiced song to the accompaniment of guitars—a simple melody, a recitative story of the war in Morocco, just now very close to everyone's heart.

> *Si me toca á mi morir encargaré á mis soldados*
> *Que rueguen á Dios por mi y sean ellos salvados.*

Another moment, and the church bells are ringing with joyous notes. Tower after tower takes up the glad refrain, until all join in the happy chorus of welcome to the noonday—the fashionable hour for Valencian señoras and señoritas to exhibit themselves on the Alameda. We take our place in the slow-moving line of automobiles, fiacres, and *tartanas*—land gondolas, they call these last, the name borrowed from a Mediterranean sailing craft having its prototype in the New England barge, which means both boat and wagon.

In single file we pass through the Torres de

IN A CATHEDRAL CHAPEL

EVERYDAY SPAIN

Serranos—one of the city's ancient gateways—
and then across the wide Turia, a river without
water, for here in Spain even rivers seem to
have caught the *mañana* spirit and keep bridges
waiting months for just a little trickle.
Stretched along this river bank is the poplar-
shaded Alameda. Already, parked side by side,
there are a hundred or so empty carriages, their
owners standing in gossiping groups or idly
sauntering along flower-hedged paths, carelessly bruising the fragrant blossoms that send
forth a soft perfume in beseeching protest.

March 17

Come with me this Friday morning into the
Iglesia del Corpus Christi. You must wear a
gown of black and cover your head with a black
mantilla, else you will not be admitted. The
unchanging church has answered the question
put by the Corinthians, "Is it comely that a
woman pray unto God uncovered?" by ordering
the faithful to appear only when wearing the
classic Spanish apparel.

The interior of the chapel is gloomily dark,
for there are no side windows and the only day-
light that can enter filters down from the dome,
which today is shrouded with heavy coverings.

Within the dim shadows spectral figures kneel in silent devotion. Only near the high altar, where soft candlelight melts the darkness, do these ghostly outlines take human form.

The sob of cellos is heard, and from out the hidden choir comes the wail of the "Miserere." Thrilling notes fill the church, and then, Ribalta's wondrous "Last Supper," above the high altar, slowly sinks from sight. Purple curtains hide the niche where it was hung. Soon these are pulled aside by unseen hands, revealing other veils—of lilac, then gray, then black. Suddenly the black veil is violently rent asunder, and within a deep recess is revealed the figure of the dying Saviour, the bent head lighted by a quivering torch.

The music ceases. Not a sound is heard save the low murmuring of prayers or the weeping of some overwrought soul.

Later

In colorful Valencia, married to pleasure, the very air seems "en fête." Ever eager for amusement, the city plays on the slightest excuse. And the desired pretext offers itself today, thanks to kindly Saint Joseph, the husband of the Blessed Virgin. According to Jewish history, many ap-

plicants sued for the hand of the Virgin. After
months of unsuccessful wooing they agreed
among themselves to put their courtship to test,
and, in accordance, left their shepherds' staffs
in the temple overnight that, perchance, a sign
might be given. Morning found the staff belonging to eighty-year-old Joseph budded into
leaf and flowering, proving beyond question
that he was the chosen of God. So in this devout
city, as romantic as it is devout, Joseph is a
favorite Christian name, and his birthday—the
birthday of thousands of Valencians (for they
observe, not the day on which they were born,
but the birthday of the saint for whom they are
named)—is a day of great rejoicing and the
occasion of a peculiar celebration known as *Les
falles de San José.*

In one street of every district in the city is
exhibited, molded from plaster and canvas, a
life-size parody of some local abuse; or there is
a picture ridiculing some man or woman living
in the ward, whose conduct has given offense.
These are burlesques, but every figure is splendidly modeled, and the painted canvas is from
the brush of some well-known artist. All day
long a merry, singing crowd gathers about these
strange exhibits, laughing or shouting approval

or disapproval. Exactly at midnight, to the blare of trumpets, a torch sets these effigies afire, and on their ashes, phœnix-like, arise banquet tables at which the merrymakers sit until the dawn of another day.

Tired of all the noise and confusion, we turn into the quiet street where lives the Marques de los Aguas. His palace is a sculptured marvel. Stone fruit and flowers festoon the windows, all heavily balconied and studded with long prongs of iron. On this festive night these iron prongs carry huge candles that cast weird shadows in the otherwise unlighted street. Within a brilliant circle of flaring tapers is a Virgin, on whose niche is inscribed the petition, *"Reyna Sacratisima de Rosaro, Rogad por Nosotros"* (Pray for us).

May she do so for you, as well as for us.

March 18

With the red and yellow flag of Spain fluttering from our radiator top and with a noise from the wide-open exhaust like the sputter from a battery of machine guns, we roar out of Valencia, bringing consternation in our wake almost as great as did the Cid when he sallied forth through the city gate for the last time.

86

The Cid, you remember, died at Valencia, just as King Bocar besieged the city with a host of followers so great that not a man in the world could count them. But Ximena, his faithful wife, as all genuine women when faced with trouble, proved equal to the emergency. Hiding her personal sorrow, she made the same preparations to meet the danger as would her husband, had he been alive. The dead body of the Cid was anointed from head to foot with myrrh and balsam, and their virtues were so great that the flesh remained firm and fair, retaining its natural color. They clothed him in noble robes and placed him upon a splendid saddle, firmly fastened to his horse Babieca, so that he sat erect. A shield was hung about his neck, and the famous sword "Tizona" was placed in his hand.

The great gate was swung open, and with the Cid in the lead they went forth followed by beasts of burden, so that nothing of price was left in the city. When the Moorish hordes saw this fearless knight of great stature seated on his white horse, a battle banner in one hand, a sword in the other, they were mightily afraid and fled, and nothing more was seen of them save dust clouds, riderless horses, and overturned tents.

But dust clouds cannot hide, and no language fit to print can describe, the century-old petrified horrors over which we plunge and flounder. However, Valencia's famous huerta, rich, warm, red-brown, lovely under the blue splendor of dawn, outstretches before us compensatingly. It is a vale of plenty, which the Moor poetically called, "a bit of heaven dropped to earth." Only touch her with a plow, and she laughs with smiling crops; laughs in glorious abandon, giving forth bounties of the soil whose like is seldom seen. The bordering old sea land is cut with frequent canals into a network of rice fields, among which are scattered curiously plastered houses with heavily thatched roofs ornamented at either end by wooden crosses. And here is the oft-pictured river Júcar, today a ribbon of water, sluggishly crawling. But when this azure sky begins to frown and in anger deluges the earth, the Júcar will rise with frightful rapidity, sweeping the countryside in ravaging torrents. Then the terror-stricken people will hasten to the parish church, seize their image of the Virgin, and dip her holy forehead into the raging waters, that they may be calmed.

The plain disappears and rugged weather-worn heights show themselves in the distance, beginning to unwind their cloud veils at the touch of early sunshine. Shouldering up one steep side is Játiba, the city that had the questionable honor of cradling the too celebrated family of Borgia, of whom Pope Alexander Borgia's natural children, the clever, inhuman Cæsar and his equally clever sister, the wanton Lucretia, were the most infamous. But Játiba amply redeemed herself by giving birth to Ribera, that celebrated painter of emaciated saints with hollow eyes and fleshless cheeks, whose faces always bear the imprint of torture and illness and weariness of life. It is said in his defense that Ribera never loved, and "life unloving is hell."

Hardly outside Játiba and we stop at a wayside thatched cottage, which the chauffeur proudly proclaims the home of his uncle. A tanner of skins is this uncle, apparently, as several fresh and bloody specimens hang about the dining table where we are seated—for politeness forbids our making use of the emergency luncheon provided by the hotel. We must satisfy our hunger with raw tomatoes and sausages, washing them down with the wine of the country, which, to save glasses, is served in clay carafes. In addition to the usual opening at the top, these carafes have a long, pointed spout projecting from the side. One is supposed to lift this strange decanter to the level of the head and pour the wine directly into the mouth without touching the lips to the nozzle end. Impossible without long practice, and our kindly host, recognizing the difficulty, brings out bowls, in which on one side of the inside is painted a fiery picture of the devil, his head almost touching the brim's edge. The extreme bottom is lettered in gilt with the words, "Jesús y María." The secret charm of this ingenious tankard lies in the fact that, if you are a good Catholic, you are expected to fill the bowl brimming full in order to drown the devil, and then, after reverently crossing yourself, drink until the words "Jesús y María" can plainly be seen. We can conscientiously recommend this, owing to the quickness of our own conversion, to all missionaries as a splendid means of proselyting.

From now on, is a continual zigzagging upwards, until we look down upon the blue of the Mediterranean, separated from the mountains by a series of scarred gashes. Doré in his maddest visioning saw nothing like it. On the downward serpentine road is the village of Santa Faz (face), far famed as treasuring one of the three handkerchiefs with which Saint Veronica wiped the face of the Saviour.

Alicante is close to the shore. Here nature has scooped a big hollow in the coast, shooting far into the sea two protecting arms that form a splendid bay. But nature planned too grandly for puny man, and in imitation he has built two tentacles of stone that now hold within their folds only a small part of this Titan harbor. From the sea-washed ends an understanding eye can encircle a panorama claimed by much-traveled Baedeker to be without parallel in all of Europe. Outstretched in the center is Alicante, the dream of summer-scorched Madrid. She seems like some oriental beauty deeply reddened by the rouge of the sun. With her feet dangling in the water, she leans against the mountain heights on whose bosom rests the cathedral church. Here beats the fiercely religious heart of this Eastern maid, while the castle on the misty peak above is her clever-working brain.

Exhausted by the sunshine that pours down in white and dazzling heat, Alicante's eyes turn longingly southward to the high parasols of a thousands palms, shielding others far less fair. Within view is dark-toned Elche, an African oasis of lofty date trees suffering the sun only to play tricks with shadows thrown upon the ground by the swaying fronds. The trees are so close together as just to permit glimpses of distant low, white-plastered houses windowed by narrow slits that are overhung with mats of rush, that do their best to hold the sun at bay. Thousands, hundreds of thousands, of date palms crowd around the city walls. As straight as the columns of a cathedral are some of these palms; others are bent forward as though graciously nodding one to the other. Many have their tufted top bound into cone shapes, so tightly corded as to cut off the circulation of sap. This turns the leaves to a bloodless white, and once bleached, they will be blessed by priests and on Palm Sunday carried in sacred procession.

From the murky depths of this almost impenetrable forest one seems to hear the weird tom-tom of native drums. The catlike, dark-hued figures clambering up the knobby trunks but confirm the impression. These *hortelanas,* with bare feet pressed hard against the tree to which they are loosely fastened by an encircling rope, quickly scale the ninety-foot giants.

Several of the finest plantations are gifts, belonging to Elche's "Lady of the Assumption," whose huertas, according to story, are prudishly allowed to have but one male tree. Outrivaling even Solomon "with his seven hundred wives and three hundred princesses and concubines," this vigorous old fellow shakes the dust of flowers over the heads of his vast arboreal harem, which eternally blossoms with rich golden fruit.

Interesting is the chronicle of this miraculous "Virgin of Elche." It relates that in the year 1370 a patrol of fishermen who were guarding the beach of the little seaport town of Santa Pola, not far distant from Alicante, discovered a large wooden box drifting with the tide. On bringing it ashore they saw to their amazement that it was labeled in still decipherable letters, *"Soy para Elche"* (I belong to Elche). This chest of cedar was found to contain an image of the Virgin Mary, and at her feet, wrapped in folds of silk, were the ancient words and music in praise of her death and assumption. Every year on the thirteenth of August is sung in Elche's cathedral this sacred passion drama, with the "stage properties" the same today as centuries ago. A blue cloth representing the celestial regions covers the ceiling, from which, caught with golden cords, depend little lace-draped angels who chant the heavenly refrains to the music of their tiny harps. An angelic boy of twelve responds for the Virgin in a divine soprano, while the "Chorus of the Blest" intone the melody.

At nightfall we turn our back on Alicante. The last rays of a crimson sun are fading into a deep, starry dusk. The dreamy waters of the Mediterranean, along which purrs our faithful car, whisper musically to the palm-shadowed shores. Mists like burning incense rise from the heated ground, giving hazy outline to the beaches where lie a huddled collection of fishing craft shrouded in their night clothes, fast asleep in beds of sand. As the heaven loses its color, a soft gray merges sky and sea together, and shortly the silvery moon pushes its way above the horizon, transforming our world into a fairyland of pearl and opal, turning the salt beds of neighboring lagoons into filmy handkerchiefs of white.

If ever angels watch over a land lovely with rest, it must be on this night. In the wayside curtainless rooms illumined by the searching light of the moon, we see children side by side on the floor, sleeping very peacefully. And if the drowsy youngsters have forgotten to mumble their usual bedside prayer—"Make the wicked Satan keep away. God is with me and I with God. Give me peace here, and after death, Paradise"—the good mother will surely have tiptoed to their side to throw a few drops of holy water over the beds, that no harm may come to them during the dark hours.

Out of the blackness, twinkling lights like a colony of fireflies come to meet us, and under the veiling cloak of darkness we enter Carthagena.

March 20

Carthagena sleeps.

A noisy peal of bells rings out first mass. It comes pouring into our rooms, to be followed by the murmurings of a city reluctantly bestirring itself. We catch the sound of quick-tapping little hoofs to the accompaniment of tinkling bells. Mingled with it is the shrill cry of goatherds urging their stubborn charges along their milky way, bringing, perhaps, to still sleepy Carthagena visions of green fields and country lanes. Across the nearly deserted plaza the faithful animals trot in single file, or some rest uncomplainingly on the hard pavements, as if in their home pastures. In turn comes a herd of cows, to whose tails are tied

playful calves. Then a string of she-asses bray-
ing furiously, protesting against giving up their
last drop of milk. In this country, as one wit
puts it, "they milk anything—even strangers."
Now around the corner rambles a street car
without a single passenger, as though taking a
stroll for pleasure. On the Calle Mayor, that
by noontime will be throbbing with life, there is
only a faint shuffling of slippered feet tardily
hurrying to mass.

Carthagena still sleeps.

From the ruins of the Castillo de la Concep-
ción atop the volcanic cliffs, the city greets us in
early morning dishabille, frowsy toilers publicly preparing for the work of another day.
Everything looks unwashed and unkempt. But
suddenly a magician's wand smites the heavens,
and above the sea the sky is flushed with crimson. Like some immense red seal the sun comes
into view, bathing and dressing the city with
golden light so powerful that even the sea gulls
stagger into the air after one single draught.
Fortresses glower at us from in front, fortresses
frown at us from the right and from the left;
for this is Spain's arsenal, with still rather antiquated defenses. If you ever become classical
enough to scan the Latin of Polybius, who spent

many months here with Scipio in B.C. 151, you will be able to read an interesting and exact account of the city.

And Carthagena still sleeps.

In the dreamy hours of noon while the land of *mañana* is again dozing, we ride our way through groves of glorious-hued oranges, where the white houses of the *cortijos* (farms) are overshadowed by groups of palms. The scene carries one back into that patriarchal poetic world pictured in early Bibles. But the face of this land, like the faces of its people, changes quickly, and the scene shifts to a wild and rugged country of savage mountain peaks and grim-looking chasms, changing again in turn into smiling meadows that surround Murcia. This "frying pan of Spain" is so hot that its priests of old, in describing Paradise, painted it as a country full of glaciers, where the angel inhabitants passed their time in sipping ice-cold drinks. The sun certainly has dried up all initiative, and the Murcians lag somewhat behind their awakening neighbors. An oft-told story has it that when Adam obtained permission to revisit the earth, he wandered from country to country in vain search of his lost Eden. On reaching Murcia, he found to his joy that

97

nothing had changed, and recognized it as his own.

In the *Ermita de Jesús* time seems to have stood still. Life is the same today as yesterday, and will be the same tomorrow. As we sign the visitors' book, the lay brother looks at us almost distrustfully, hardly believing it possible we could have come from so great a distance. "I have never been away from here," he says, somewhat sadly, "and there is the friend with whom I live," pointing to a ghastly crucifix of Christ, bleeding dark-red wax, a gruesome sight.

Scarcely preparation, this, for the splendid processional figures for which the hermitage is celebrated. With what infinite pains and loving care the sculptor Salzillo carved these lifelike statues. It is told of him that he labored many long, weary months over the single figure of Our Lady of Sorrows, never able to chisel on the face of the Virgin the agony of grief that filled her soul on the death of her blessed son. As a last resort, he handed his own daughter a forged letter, telling of the suicide of her lover, watching, with modeling tools in hand, as she read. His joy was very great when he thus caught the long-desired expression and was able to finish this wonderful statue.

The city lies quivering in the embrace of an ardent sun, whose acid sharp rays burn in the plate of memory a coquettish etching of Murcia's fair ones, as, with fans fluttering like the wings of so many butterflies, they saunter along the shadeless river, vainly seeking some cooling breeze.

5

Granada, City of Mystery

"Fortuna" was kind when she merged our path with that of Manuel the artist. How could he help being an artist! "I was born in the Palace of the Alhambra," he says, "and from childhood to manhood spent all my days within its glories.

"My age? You ask, Señor, because my hair is white, while my face is young. I am only thirty, but like Boabdil, the last of Granada's sultans, I seem always to have been unlucky. Just as for him 'those daughters of night, the Fates, spun pitfalls for my feet, closing my eyes so that I might not see them.' The first sorrow came when, after sixty years of faithful wardenship, my father, 'the dog of the Alhambra,' was forced out by an ingrate government who wished the post for some fawning favorite. On foot we journeyed to Madrid, hoping for an interview with the King, remembering his visit to the palace under my father's guidance and the promise made while there. It was in the Patio

100

del Mexuar where there is a panel of marble badly warped. 'How did that happen?' asked the King. Without thought my father replied, 'It was picked too green.' The courtiers were horrified, but the King burst into laughter, patted my father on the back, and said, 'My good fellow, I shall never forget you.'

"But the King did forget, and my father died of a broken heart.

"Several years ago I wandered back to Granada, and today I try to help others to feel and love the beauties of my old home."

So it is that Manuel sits by our side. As we hurry along, the country unfolds like some gigantic album whose leaves are being turned, one by one. And Manuel claps his hands with Latin enthusiasm at each of Nature's inimitable canvases. The first shows the garden land of Murcia, smiling under the scorching sun at her much-spoiled children, to whom, without trouble, come all the fruits of the earth. And on the very next page is shown a country arid and parched, whose only green thing is the cactus of a thousand prickles. Then follow harsh gray mountains, where Nature reveals herself in savage mood. There are dozens of smaller portraits clamoring for attention, each as charming as the other; the one just seen, so alluring as not only to efface regret for so hurriedly passing the first, but urging us on toward the next.

Muleteers pass and repass, chanting a sad rhythm borrowed from the Arabs, and from the fields below comes floating, in minor key, the same strange, tragic song. It was very near by, as Lope de Vega relates in his celebrated drama, that the Arabs and Christians fought with such horrible carnage that the land was crimsoned with blood. These pathetic chants picture the ghostly armies battling with one another and tell how Christian steel beat down the flashing scimitar.

As is usual with many boundary lines in Spain, a cross marks the entrance into the Province of Andalusia. This province, according to popular belief, was granted to Santa Lucia by Saint James (Santiago), who was the elect of the Apostles to preach the gospel in Spain, and who became Spain's patron saint and arbitrator.

Now it came to pass that Santa Lucia was the only saint in heaven who did not possess some country over which she might reign. She was most unhappy, grieving for many years, until kindly Saint James heard of her sorrow and, to comfort her, said she might go to his country,

Spain, and choose any part she liked. Down to earth she hurried, entering Spain by its northern gateway. But finding it cold and bleak, she turned toward the south, toiling through desert and mountain land in a vain search. At length one day, from the high peak of Sierra de María, she saw the country of her dreams, and she heard the voice of Saint James saying, *"Anda Lucia!"* (Go, Lucia!) So she went, and took the province for her own.

We are in the land of many sierras, sometimes groping blindly in dark gulfs where the waters growl; sometimes on the heights rushing through a sea of sunfire that seems to splash us as we pass; now and again catching a glimpse of the far-distant summits, with their diadems of eternal snow.

Manuel clasps his hands in a state of positive ecstasy. *"¡Veo el cielo abierto!"* (I see the heavens opening!) "After a beautiful woman, give me a beautiful landscape," he exclaims. "What can so quickly capture the heart or the eyes!"

Just outside the city, near the little town of Purullena, the ground is strewn with hundreds of pinkish cones. Into this singular shelter, a whole village has burrowed its way. At our

103

approach, a horde of the children of Egypt, the desert in their eyes, and their faces tanned almost black by many flaming summers, spring from out their caves. At once we are surrounded by a noisy troop of ragamuffins. Their eyes sparkle with expectancy. Manuel angrily waves them away. "You don't care for children?" we ask. "Indeed I do, but I can't afford them. Happily God has protected me, and I have none."

The remainder of the way we are in the company of the snow-capped sierras, whose cold heights are wrapped within the white arms of the clouds. It grows late, and there is no real twilight in Spain. Darkness soon falls about us, and in the heavens just above the Moorish Alhambra appears a tiny crescent moon. Allah still watches over Granada.

As quickly as possible we hurry through the city streets, noisy with the usual evening crowd, and into a beautiful park of elms. Under the heavy foliage and to the music of running waters, we climb Alhambra hill, the end of this day's pilgrimage. Our balcony looks down upon the city, silvery in the moonlight, with overhead a sky of that deep purple-blue of which the Arabians were wont to say, "Allah made only just enough to cover this terrestrial paradise." We stand entranced with the almost spectral mystery. The thrilling call of the nightingale, in praise of love, comes from out the half-dark of the woods. Then all is quiet, and we are alone with our dreams.

March 22

Alas, the cold revealing light of day destroys the mystery of night. Can that possibly be the famous entrance Gate of Justice, where the people were judged with just judgment? Of such gates we read in the Old Testament, and, indeed, it was from the Hebrews the Arabs borrowed the law, "Judges shalt thou make in all thy gates." It must be that Mohammedan justice was administered here, for there above the outer gate is the well-known outstretched hand, the five fingers symbolizing the five foundation principles of the Koran: Faith in one God, Prayer, Charity, Fasting, and Pilgrimage to Mecca; while over the inner archway is the key —the key to heaven given to all believers in the Koran.

Through the winding passage so twisting as to check an entering foe, we take our way, and our eyes are greeted with Charles the Fifth's grandiose attempt to build a Roman castle on the

105

site of the dainty El Harem. Seeking to humble by mere size, proudly to compare the virility of the Spaniard with the effeminacy of the Arab, the result is an artistic crime. Never inhabited, never even finished, quite worthy it is of a monarch who never finished anything—even his own reign.

The dun brown, uninteresting walls of the Alhambra give not the slightest hint of the beauty within. It is almost impossible to realize that in the golden days they hid from vulgar gaze the most picturesque court of Europe and such pampered harems of loveliness as never will be seen again. This palace was dedicated to pleasure by the Moslem, who paints his heaven as the abode of luxurious voluptuousness. "Thou givest safety even to the blades of grass, and inspirest terror in the very stars of heaven. When the shining stars quiver, it is through dread of thee; when the grass of the fields bends down, it is to give thee thanks." So sang the Arabic poets in praise of Mohammed V, whose glory is the Alhambra.

But you must close your eyes to the drab, featureless surroundings. Give me your hand and let me lead you within. And you must come often and stay long, for only then will the

Alhambra learn to know you; not till then will it reveal itself to you, tell you its hidden secrets, as to a proven friend.

We are back in the olden days, and in imagination we enter through the garden fronting the Mexuar, pushing by the white burnoosed Moors who are solemnly stalking through the orange-bordered paths, impatiently awaiting their turn to settle some dispute, or in expectation of the long-delayed answer to some petition. Within the Mexuar is a wrangling, gesticulating mob of bearded Turks, swarthy, yellow-slippered Arabs, and equally swarthy Jews. The noise and confusion is momentarily stilled only when some of the disputants are taken by the presiding Cadi to the adjoining santuario where, within the Mihrâb, looking to the east, they swear on the Koran and by the beard of Mahomet to fulfill their pledges. With clanking steel an officer shoulders his way through the crowd, and from the fountained patio beyond he passes into the winding Zaguán, where guards bar the passage except to members of the household. Into the same patio two magnificently robed vizirs are ushered with ceremonious salaams. But they turn to the left, into the Cuarto Dorado, the antechamber of the throne room. There they hastily withdraw to the farthest corner for a final consultation, not knowing that over their heads is a movable tile which, at the press of a button, opens just enough to carry the faintest whisper to listening ears. If their speech be treasonous, the heads of the two grand vizirs will soon roll at the feet of the waiting Sultan.

It was out of the window of this room, over-looking the precipitous banks of the Darro, that the Sultana Aisha let her son, Boabdil, down with a rope made of shawls, that he might escape from the Sultan Muley Abu'l-Hassan, who was about to sacrifice him to the intrigues of her rival, Morning Star. Far better for him had he remained, and met death with his brothers!

Despite the African guards who, with gleam-ing daggers in their hands, sit within the two dusky alcoves, we follow, in our waking dream, the same twisting passage as did the officer before us. As we enter the Court of Myrtles, the great doors swing open to admit the grand dignitaries granted audience with the Sultan. A quick shuffling of slippered feet can be heard on the screened balcony above, whence curious feminine eyes excitedly peer through at the splendor of color as the magnificently costumed pashas, viceroys, governors, and grand officers

MIRADOR DE DARAXA, THE ALHAMBRA.

COURT OF MYRTLES, THE ALHAMBRA.

walk the length of the patio up to the Sala de la
Barca. Many times they kneel, advancing but
a few steps after each genuflection, for through
the archway can be seen the awful presence of
the Sultan, surrounded by his courtiers, in dazzling white turbans and plumed casques heavy
with gems. Just where the fairy frescoes weave
the words "Thou art the center of the palace as
the heart is the center of the body," sits the Sultan, with face of marble. His hands seemingly
play with his silky beard, but in reality they are
prepared to signal in case of need to the two
guards who stand sentinel, their eyes constantly
fixed on their master, ready to spring at the
slightest sign. Nine great embrasures, the thick-
ness of the massive walls, give light filtered
through leaded windows of cathedral glass.
Immense bronze lamps burning scented oil
hang from the domed ceiling, an imitation of
the vault of heaven. Gold and silver tissues are
strewn about the floor, and on the walls are
hangings of jeweled embroideries fringed with
pearls.

So it was when Boabdil called his ministers
together in council to discuss the answer to be
made the Catholic kings who had sent a herald
with terms of surrender. Only one minister

dared advise resistance, saying to Ferdinand's herald, "Does the Christian King think us women, that we should yield with swords in our hands? Far better to an African is a grave in the ruins of the Alhambra than the richest couch in his proudest palace." But the others wept, and Boabdil signed the agreement, thereby dooming himself to everlasting opprobrium. Even today his tombstone is the sill of a doorway into a public bath, that all of the faithful passing in and out shall trample upon the memory of the man who lost for the children of the Prophet their fairest possession.

In this Court of Myrtles—flower best loved of the Moors, for does not the Koran say, "Thou wil'st have no peace at home until the myrtle is planted"?—masses of its vivid green hem in a pool of clear water. Within its cool depths are mirrored the exquisite arches whose slender marble columns support the galleries and sleeping apartments of the women of the court, while reflected almost at our feet is the Tower of Comares.

The side walls enclosing the pool are pierced with latticed windows that give light to the quarters of the serving women. Beneath are doors that open into the rooms of the palace eunuchs. Large tiled alcoves—*al-hanîja*—offer rest to the officers of the day, and small niches at the doorways, relief to the thirsty. "He who comes to me tortured with thirst will find water pure and fresh, sweet and unmixed."

But only in the heart of the harem are to be found the inner secrets of the Orient, and for them we turn to the Court of Lions.

One playful Sunday a party of plundering Moors seized five maidens at the fountain of a Christian village and brought them into Granada for sale. According to law, a fifth of the "plunder" belonged to the Sultan, and he, of course, chose the most beautiful—a maiden so fair that she is known as the Morning Star. With the other odalisks of the harem, she was walking one day in the warmth of the afternoon, as was her wont, under these shaded arches. Slender maids all, lending their eyes in furtive glances at the Sultan watching from out his private apartment. Suddenly a handkerchief fluttered in the air and fell at the feet of Morning Star, signifying that she was the chosen one. She bowed to earth, picked up the handkerchief, and placed it in her bosom in token of submission. At midnight, dressed in superb silks and adorned with jewels, she was con-

III

ducted by musicians playing psalteries to the room of the Sultan, where, falling on her knees, she timidly approached and lifted the gold-brocaded covering at the foot of the couch that she might kiss the feet of her lord and master.

Dark-eyed Zorayah captured the heart of her sovereign, Muley Abu'l-Hassan, and reigned until his death. The poets of that day sing of her hair as golden threads, her eyes as two resplendent suns, her cheeks pure damask rose, her teeth pearls, her lips rubies, and her neck alabaster. We see her reclining at ease on rich, soft cushions, indolently watching the dancing of slaves to the languorous music of harps and lutes. But with one glance revealing that the Sultan is dissatisfied, she springs to her feet and dances, herself, that she may give pleasure to her lover and make him desire her the more. In those days woman's charms were physical, and the swaying motion of the dance, with the sunlight striking through diaphanous drapery, revealed the deep olive hue of her lithe, sinuous body.

But Christian Zorayah was as clever as she was beautiful. She declared that if the Church taught that a woman must be ignorant to attain heaven, she would prefer hell. It was her

clever schemes that brought trouble between the
rival ruling factions, leading to the final disrup-
tion of the Moorish kingdom.

The Court of Lions is a palace of lace, of airy
pavilions and galleries, of deep niches painted
in pale blues and faded terra cottas, of embroidered ceilings, of fountains that splash their
waters against the silence; and everywhere, for
him that hath the eyes to read and the heart and
mind to receive, are poetic messages. Over the
doorway, "Delicately have the fingers of the
artist embroidered my robe after setting the
jewels of my diadem." Within the entrance,
"You are like the bright moon that casts forth
his light over the face of heaven." While above
the archaic lions that crouch in stiff, uncouth
poses, one may read, "Is this a fountain that
flows, or is it the tears of some hopeless admirer
of the fair maid who, covered with pearls, walks
in this garden of love?"

The marvelous ceiling of the "Two Sisters"
is a mass of pendent stalactites, an emblematic
beehive of a thousand cells wrought in the very
colors of the flowers. Here the soul of the queen
bee should find the Moorish heaven which gives
supremacy to women.

It is related that when this exquisite jewel box

was finished, all but the ceiling, which was plain and unsatisfactory, the disconsolate architect went alone to commune with Mahomet upon his difficulty. Suddenly there danced into the room a bevy of concubines, who began to pelt one another with snowballs that had been brought down from the high sierra for their amusement. Now and again they would hit the ceiling instead of the person at whom they aimed, as is woman's wont, and the snow clinging to the ceiling would gradually melt into the form of icicles. This so amused the maidens that they continued to throw at the ceiling instead of at one another. The architect had received his answer from Allah.

But the crowning feature of this room is its multitude of arches, terminating in a window once open to a wide sweep over the river Darro and up to the mighty sierras. It is all like some idyllic tent raised in a desert oasis. Indeed, the abode of the nomad Arab was its inspiration, for from the tent, it is said, all oriental architecture got its inspiration. The thin and fragile marble columns were in imitation of tent poles; the carpets with which the tents were draped find their echo in the brilliant colors of filmy pattern. The arches reproduce the turbans of their occupants, and the drooping capitals of the pillars picture the leaves of palms.

From the window of the arches such a picture now fills the sky as some favorite of the Sultan may often have dreamed over from this very casement. The summits of the mountains are in the midst of a mighty conflagration. Soon the sinking sun tints the peaks to a delicate rose color and pearls the slopes with every shade on the palette of God.

March 23

Today we walk through gardens once shaded by the feathery foliage of the tamarisk. It was the sweet juice of this fruit that, on hardening, was gathered by the Arabs and pressed into cakes called "manna." Soon we reach the Torre de las Damas (Women's Tower), and there, open to the sky, but shielded from view by stiff hedges, is a pool of quiet water in which, under the watchful eyes of dark-visaged eunuchs, oriental beauties used to bathe. Over the open court the golden sun would cast a luminous crown, adorning the olive-skinned maidens as they sat by the water's edge combing out their lustrous black tresses, and vitalizing the Persian inscription over the doorway, "You are like the

115

rainbow when it shines, and the sun is your lord." After the bath, these languid beauties would rest within the tiny patio upon soft, luxurious cushions laid over pierced marble slabs from which arose the incense of Eastern perfumes, listening, the while, to the music of lutes played in the balconies above.

Saunter with me around the fortress walls that in former days were defended by twenty-three towers. The faded brown silhouette of a few can still be seen. Some are the setting for the daintiest and most delicately colored plaster fantasies in all the Alhambra; others are merely fortified places, with quarters for guards and roof lookouts. It was from these very lookouts that, for so many anxious months, the Arabs sadly watched the Spaniards stripping off bit by bit the outer rind of the pomegranate (Granada), devouring it seed by seed until they reached the luscious pith so aptly symbolized in the delights of the Alhambra Palace. It took eight long months, and legend curiously relates that Queen Isabella had taken an oath never to change her chemise until Granada fell—from which comes the present-day name of "Isabel" for a certain yellow linen.

At the Torre de la Cautiva (Tower of the

Captive) let all good Christians uncover and repeat the prayer for the repose of the soul, for, from the screened window overlooking the foaming Darro, the lovely Catholic lady, Isabel da Lara, taken prisoner by the Moors, threw herself to death to avoid the attentions of her madly infatuated captor, Aben-Muhamed. To gain time, in the hope of rescue, Isabel told the impetuous Moor that she could not bring herself to marry a Mohammedan, but that if he would embrace Christianity, she would then become his wife. He left Granada and was taken secretly into the Catholic Church, returning to the tower for his anticipated reward. That same day, Isabel's Christian lover, Ponce de Leon, had organized an expedition of his hotheaded young friends from the camp at Santa Fé. They managed to surprise the tower. De Leon killed Aben-Muhamed, but was himself killed by the Moor's body servant, who, in turn, died at the hands of De Leon's friends. In the one small tower room three lay dead, and at the foot of the tower lay another body—that of the girl whose rescuers had arrived just one hour too late to save her.

We hurry by the Torres de los Picos, de las Infantas, and del Candil, not stopping until the

Puerta de los Siete Suelos is reached. Through this gateway the grief-stricken Boabdil rode forth from the Alhambra, *"¡Ay! nunca, nunca más verla!"* (Alas! never, never more to see it!) Rather fittingly, it would seem, it was at the foot of the Hill of Martyrs, in whose caves more than thirty thousand Christian slaves had been chained while toiling for the Moors in building the palace, that the victorious Spanish army awaited him. Isabella and Ferdinand, also on horseback, were there surrounded by the nobles and chivalry of Castile and Aragon. Up to the waiting victors rode the discrowned Sultan. Hastily dismounting, he tendered the precious keys of the fortress to the conquerors. "They are thine, O King, since Allah so decrees, but be merciful as you are strong. One last favor I implore, destroy the gate through which I left, that no man henceforth shall see the path of my desertion." They promised, and today the Puerta de los Siete Suelos lies in ruins.

When Boabdil had saluted Isabella and had kissed the hand of Ferdinand, the Christian procession, in magnificent array and with pennants flying, moved toward the heights singing psalms of thanksgiving. As the procession reached the Plaza de los Aljibes, a silver cross blazed from the Torre de la Vela, the crimson and golden flag of Spain beside it, fluttering over the crescent banner which was slowly withdrawn. To the triumphant shouts of the heralds, "Santiago, Castellar, Granada," and to the ringing of bells, Ferdinand and his followers knelt to chant the Te Deum, the King crying aloud, "Not for ourselves, O Lord, not for ourselves, but for thy glory!"

To the Christians the Alhambra belongs, but in far-away Africa every Friday prayers are still offered for the recovery of this terrestrial paradise.

March 24

Last night we went to see the gypsies dance. We crossed the river Darro where, on a steep mountain spur, is the rocky Albaicín, once "the sister and rival of the proud palace hill," but today the quarters of the gypsies, faithful to nothing except their own interest. Not, however, quite a true statement in all senses of the word "faithful," for while probably no race is more licentious in word, dance, and gesture, the women are one and all corporeally chaste, having from early youth some lazy husband of their own people, most of whom, lizard-like, are sprawling on the rocks, doing nothing. And it is perhaps worth noting that all the women of Spain, thanks to the Church and a life of comparative seclusion, are freer from liaisons than those of any country in Europe.

Along the road at the base of this sacred mountain the rocks are honeycombed with cave dwellings overgrown with coarse cactus. They are the present home of some of the Egyptians who are scattered over the face of the earth; "coming from no man knows whence; going no man knows thence," a curse set upon them at the time they cast out Joseph and Mary, who had sought refuge in Egypt.

We enter one of the whitewashed hovels. Around the wall awaiting us are seated a dozen sun-scorched *gitanos*. Some are veritable witch-hags, even the heavy rouge and powder barely concealing the wrinkles engraved by the fingers of age. A few are strangely bewitching—supple, tall, and dark-eyed, their blue-black hair tumbling in ringlets about their cheeks, the kind of woman that might fetter a man with degrading passion.

Castanets and tambourines strike the opening note. All rise. Guitars join in with languorous chords, and the *casamiento gitano* (the gypsy

THE GYPSY QUARTER OF GRANADA.

GRANADA. BEYOND, THE ALHAMBRA AND SIERRA NEVADA.

marriage dance) is begun. It starts gravely and slowly, with mysterious smiles and lowered eyelids. The rhythm at first is sad; soon, however, it turns gay. The movements of the dancers quicken, the hands serpentine up and down along the body as though trying to picture the hidden form. The half-closed eyes open wide, and a devilish light shines in the black pupils.

There is a mad clapping of hands, furious cries of *"¡Oye! ¡Oye!"* The tambours clash excitedly, guitars sound with bizarre note, and the bodies of the dancers respond in violent, passionate motion; the hips yield, the waist twists, the shoulders almost touch the ground, and the dance ends in a breathless whirl of folly.

Dance succeeds dance, *fandango* succeeds *tarantela; jota,* the *cachucka*—all suggestive, perhaps, but never vulgar.

While the spirit of Granada lingers on Alhambra Hill, the material body lives in the town below, amid mechanical pianos and gramophones on stilts, raining harsh music on ears tuned to the soft sounds of guitars. The city is casting off her medieval attire and donning modern garments, straightening the crookedness of her streets and tearing down the storied buildings of the past. Even the interior stone of the cathedral has been scraped and cleaned until it looks as though put in place yesterday instead of in 1523.

Cold and lacking in soul, unsympathetic to prayer and sorrow is the cathedral of Granada. The effect striven for seems to have been grandeur, to which all else is subservient. Everything is massive, whether executed by Juan de Maeda, the favorite pupil of Diego de Siloe, or by the master architect himself.

Strange chance brought these two men together. While Diego was hard at work, a man unknown to him approached, demanding work. Harassed by many applications of the same sort, the master impatiently pointed to a block of stone and bade the newcomer prove his worth by carving it. "What shall I carve?" was asked. "Anything! Anything!" cried Diego, striving to answer half a dozen questions at one and the same time. "But master, what shall I carve?" the man insisted. "Oh, the devil!" exclaimed the master, striding away.

Juan de Maeda accordingly carved the devil. When Diego saw the work, he gazed at it with amazement. "What's this?" "Your order." The master examined the carving more closely.

" 'Tis devilishly well done," he said, laughing, "and I promise you a place for it in the cathedral." Whereupon the master himself set to work upon the other side of the same stone and out of it he carved his Ecce Homo—the Holy Christ of the Puerta del Colegio—with the devil at the back.

But it is Alonso Cano who has richly peopled the cathedral with masterful statues and tender paintings. Unweariedly he slaved for the church that had offered him refuge in its belfry tower after Madrid had banished him—a complete cripple except for his right hand, which had been saved by the King's expressed command. Said the King, "If he survives the torture of the rack," on which he was stretched in an effort to make him confess the suspected murder of his wife, "let him be able to continue painting.

Historically the glories of the cathedral are the tombs of Ferdinand and Isabella and of their daughter, Juana the Mad, and her husband, Philip the Handsome, united at least in death. Their effigies in armor and white marble robes lie on gorgeous catafalques, marvels of exquisite workmanship. But they themselves sleep in the dim obscurity of a dingy vault, in simple leaden coffins, giving the lie to the splendor and magnificence above.

My God, how lonely are the dead!

April 1

As we linger for a moment a mile or so beyond the city walls to wave a last *adios* to Granada, "the widowed capital of the Moor," our awakened curiosity voices itself in question. Why, O City of Mystery, did you call yourself Granada? Will the world ever know? Is it because you rest on four hills, that are like the four quarters of the "fire-opal pomegranate," *granada* in Spanish? If we conjecture aright, you did well, having the eye of a prophet that foresaw the misfortunes to come, for the sorrows of your ill-fated children are perfectly symbolized by the pomegranate, that in ripening age bleeds and bleeds as from a cut in the human heart.

Do our eyes see more than reality? Who dares deny the lingering presence of the spirits of the armies of the Crescent who, times innumerable, swept these plains with shouts of "No God but Allah!" But when the phantom hosts of Spain challenged, Allah forsook them, and those ruined watchtowers on the lower

ranges that curve about the city flashed un-
answered and in vain their fire signals for help.

Then it was that sad-faced Boabdil, with the
resigned expression of a man born to ill luck,
sought the wild sierras for safety, accompanied
by a still faithful band of black-skinned Ethiopians. His mother, Aisha, and the large-eyed
Sultana, closely guarded by mutes and eunuchs,
followed after, garbed in robes of death and
bearing ashes on their heads. When the sorrowful procession reached the little knoll not far
from the neighboring village of Alhendin, the
ill-starred Sultan turned for a last look at the
fair city he had lost, tears streaming down his
face.

"You do well," scoffed his stern and resolute
mother,—far more a man than he,—"to weep
like a woman for what you could not defend like
a man."

"Allah Achba!" cried the fugitive monarch.
"When were woes ever equal to mine!" And
the knoll where Boabdil wept is to-day called *El
Ultimo Suspiro del Moro,* "The Last Sigh of
the Moor."

6

Cordova, Ancient Mecca of the West

Across the river bordering our road is Santa
Fé, the City of Sacred Faith, the only town in
Spain wherein a Moorish foot has never trod.
It was born of a fire that burned the tent of Isabella the Catholic. Not a tent, says the chronicle, but an oriental pavilion made of sheets of
golden cloth, with silver lances for the supporting columns and brocaded velvet for curtains.
It burned so quickly that the Queen had barely
time to escape, and so the King built a city of
solid stone and mortar wherein she should be
safe. This poor little town, with regular monotonous streets like some Roman camp, was the
stage for two of the most moving dramas of a
dramatic epoch—the signing of the surrender
of Granada that gave back to Spain its old possessions, and the sealing of a contract with Columbus that brought to Spain a new world.

We pass the Pinos-Puente, the selfsame bridge
over which Columbus was doggedly journeying
on his way to France after having been rejected
by Spain as a vain dreamer, when he was over-

taken by the Queen's courier. "Stop! The Queen has sent me. She bids you to return unto Santa Fé, saying she will favor your plans." And the tall, thin-faced man who knew how to wait with the patience of genius, wept for very joy.

The mountains of Parapanda are losing themselves in the mists, and Manuel, who is still with us, dubiously shakes his head, quoting the local proverb that "When Parapanda's brow is hid, it rains, though God Himself forbid." But for once he is wrong. All day long we "eat the sun," its blazing heat, however, happily tempered by a wind born in the snowy mountains. The whitewashed villas resemble so many sails skimming the surface of this vega-like sea.

Granada at length disappears, and hill succeeds hill, as on the ocean one wave follows another. The villages seem deaf and dumb, for the sun which tinges their low, square buildings a brilliant ocher has driven everyone within doors, and the silence is broken only by the song of waters from the old fountains in the quiet squares.

More mountains, now the bleak color of steel, wrought into whimsical shapes that rise like a savage cry into the profaned heavens. One of

the far-distant peaks is that Peña de los Enamo-
rados, from which the two eloping lovers unable to escape their pursuing parents threw
themselves, locked in each other's arms—an episode that Southey immortalized in "Laila and
Manuel."

Very far apart are the towns, like shipwrecks
lost in the forgotten harbor of these far-away
mountain corners. Life here must be a melancholy thing of deadening monotony. The people live on in endless toil—and at their deaths,
others are born to the same plodding routine.
Are they content, shall we ever know? Probably we shall not, for beneath the courteous grace
of these people is an Eastern reserve hiding their
inner thoughts.

We are approaching the plains of Cordova.
A long stretch of golden corn mixed with poppies of violent red extends to the very foot of the
Sierra de Cordova, the mountain guardians of
the city. On their cloudy heights we can dimly
distinguish the ruins of that gorgeous palace
built for the fair favorite, Az-Zahrâ, a palace
of such insolent, voluptuous splendor that its like
has never been seen. It cost the then enormous
sum of seven million pieces of gold—money left

the Sultan by his wife to ransom Moslem prisoners. The widowed Sultan, on searching throughout the land, was unable to find a single Moslem captive; so he conceived the comforting thought of expending the money on a palace for his favorite, in whose society he might hope to forget his grief. But the Christian Az-Zahrâ wept on seeing its splendor, saying that the snowy marble enclosed by somber brown hills was like a white captive in the arms of a Moor. The unfortunate Sultan answered nothing, but within a year the hills were covered with almond trees whose blossoms whitened the countryside for miles around, filling the air with wind-swept flowers that fluttered to earth in snowy flakes.

Later

We have reached Cordova. In the soft darkness of early spring, we wander through the city's shadowy streets. Their silence is filled with excited anticipation, and wherever the veils of darkness are spread most thickly, we find the natural children of this sensuous night of sweet perfume—two lovers. The man is motionless against the solid iron window grating which unsympathetic parents have raised as a bar to too fervent courtship, forgetting that youth laughs at restraining bars and that bolts seldom lock out love's catastrophes.

Behind the *reja,* the girl, embarrassed at our presence, shrinks back, melting into the dusk. We hurry away, leaving the street to the lovers, only to stumble against other dim figures clinging to other barred windows from which comes the murmur of voices breaking into song. In this land of romance no lover's speech is complete without some verse. One of them Manuel interprets:

"Go, now, and tell the moon she need not rise tonight,
  Or shine, because I have my comrade's eyes to give me light."

Many and many a man sees his future wife for the first time on the street. If sufficiently attracted to discover her address, he follows her home, and thereafter spends a part of each day beneath her balcony or before the heavily barred window in silent wooing. If the parents approve, some day his anxious eyes will see a little hand at the window; it throws a white blossom plucked from the starry vine that clambers the patio within; then he sees a smiling face, the dark eyes full of fire, the smile flashing a promise. The courtship has now begun in earnest. The man has received parental sanction to talk from the street, or, if the girl of his choice is fortunate enough to occupy the groundfloor apartment, they may clasp hands or pass a rose whose "touch is like the touch of a human cheek." Unhappy the girl who lives on the top floor!

Every street of this still oriental-glamored city, once the rival of ancient Bagdad, outshining even Damascus in all its glory, leads to something of beauty or to such storied experience of the spectral past that one wonders whether life is actually real.

We peer into the rickety, wooden-balconied courtyard of the Posada del Potro, which lovers of Cervantes will recognize as "the wickedest spot in Cordova."

We linger in front of a dilapidated old palace partly concealed by somber cypresses. The broad façade shows but one tiny, flickering light, that shadows the faint contour of a worn and wearied face, an old man, Manuel tells us, once exceeding rich. In the prodigal fashion of old Spain, he ruined himself in a mad display of extravagant welcome to generous, luxury-loving Isabella the Second. Respected for such self-sacrificing devotion, he is permitted to remain amid the faded splendors of his old home, where lonely and alone he awaits the time when his spirit will be called to the mercy of God.

We stand before the Torre de Mar Muerte, that mute witness to the expiation of Conde Priego for the unjust murder of his wife. A friend of the Count's fell in love with this charming lady. Although repulsed time and time again, he managed to secure the key to her private apartment, which he stealthily entered by night. The Countess indignantly drove him away, but the husband chancing to see this Don Juan leaving his wife's room, fatally wounded him and killed the unfortunate lady. Blindly groping his way out of the house, el Conde stumbled against the body of his friend, who, in a supreme effort, had crawled back to the doorstep, striving to right the wrong he had committed. Clutched in stiffening fingers was a letter from the Countess upbraiding him for his perfidy, and across one page, in the ink of his own blood, painfully traced in almost illegible letters, were his final words of amend, "I swear by the crucifix, she is innocent." But it was too late, and the husband in an agony of remorse built this prison tower, himself to be the first prisoner, and remained there until his death.

We enter the little Plaza de los Dolores,

where the velvety sky, bright with the brightness of innumerable stars, transforms the lime-white walls into sheets of silver. In the midst of this shimmering light rises a great crucifix, time-stained and blackened by wind and weather, whimsically shadowed by the feeble flames of the quaint-fashioned lamps encircling it.

It is a place of subtle beauty, whose charm is rudely broken by the noisy clatter of a wooden rattle announcing the city's watchman. Carrying an ancient spear and lantern, he strides across the square, chanting the hour and the state of the weather, *"Ave Maria Santísima, las doce son y sereno"* (Twelve o'clock and all is well). Then, as the heavy footsteps lose themselves in the darkness, and all is quiet again, a woman of the street steals in from out a dark alley and flings herself on her knees before the crucifix with passionate abandon, seeking comfort where comfort is always to be found.

April 3

"Let us raise to Allah an Aljamia which shall surpass the Temple of Jerusalem. Let us build a mosque on the site of a Christian sanctuary which we will destroy, so that we may set forth how the cross shall fall and become abased be-

133

fore the true Prophet. Allah will never give the power of the world to those who make themselves slaves of drink and lustfulness, while they preach abstinence and the joys of chastity; enriching themselves at the expense of others, while they extol poverty."

With this fierce arraignment against Christianity, the Omaiyades laid the foundation of a noble monument to the strange religion whose Koran promises a future paradise of darkskinned virgins who will mix in golden cups the forbidden wine of earth.

The Arabs, so amazingly clever in beautifying the interior of all their buildings, have little enriched the outside walls of their great mosque. It looks more like a fortress than a sanctuary, an expression of militant Mohammedanism that provides a poor binding for so sumptuous a book. A garden is its vestibule. Between rows of orange trees murmuring fountains spout water that falls in vaporous rains. It is easy to convert the modern-dressed loiterers into turban-headed Africans and swarthy, white-burnoosed Berbers who, when the voice from the muezzin tower invites to prayer, purify themselves in the fountain water, washing the nostrils, the mouth, the hands, the feet, repeating the prescribed

THE PATIO OF AN INN AT CORDOVA

INTERIOR OF THE MEZQUITA, CORDOVA.

prayers of the Koran while prostrating themselves in such deep humility that their foreheads touch the ground.

We cross the patio and enter one of the nineteen arched gateways, to find superb avenues of stone pillars continuing the aisles formed by the garden orange trees. In the subdued light it resembles another walled-in garden, and a breeze carries through it the fragrance of orange flowers. Here are no open central spaces, but a thousand jasper trees form long, straight lanes that cross and recross one another. We follow a pathway into the depths of the sacred grove, turning towards Mecca in search of the spirit of Allah, which, if anywhere, must still hover over the *Mihrâb,* glory of the mosque. The most gorgeous *Mihrâb* in all the land of Islam is this, a brilliant mosaic on gold ground, which Arabian writers poetize into "dust of stars."

A huge conch shell is the roof of this holy of holies. The floor, of marble, is deeply worn by the devotion of centuries of pilgrims who, on their knees, have made a seven-time circuit of the pearl-studded Koran written by the holy hand of Omar and sprinkled with his sacred blood. In the palmy days when the faithful came in thousands from the most remote regions to prostrate themselves before this *Mihrâb*, what a wonder the mosque must have been! Each sultan in turn added some new and rare beauty. Those were the distinguished days when Cordova was the garden of learning, the Mecca of musicians, poets, painters, and philosophers; when the Jews joined the Moors in the cultivation of the arts and sciences. Do we sometimes forget that in the dark ages, when our Saxon forefathers slept in hovels, on dirty straw, Cordova's learned Hebrews kept the torch of scholarship bright and shining, holding it in trust for future generations?

But I am wandering. Let us go back for a moment to the mosque, which Renan says he never entered without regretting that he was not a Mussulman. Its witching mystery lies largely in the unbroken vista. Break the perspective, and you destroy some of its charm—and unhappily it has been broken. In the heart of this lovely forest, fanatically tortured souls have built a pretentious cathedral, in their irreligious blindness thinking to triumph over the heretic. Religious, yes; for God is everywhere, can be worshiped anywhere, and so crude an adaptation of a mosque to Christianity has but emphasized the dreamy soul of an unknown faith.

It is in the busy, gossipy Calle del Conde de Gondomar that the current of Cordova's life pulses strongest. There nothing escapes the hungry eyes of the café loungers. The street, closed to vehicles, is their stage, the promenaders are the actors, and they, the comfortably seated audience, all with cigarettes glowing like tiny fireflies, comment audibly, with the sanction of long usage, on the passing show.

We push our way through the narrow aisles of tables under a yellow-green awning. A man courteously moves his glass, that we may share his place. What a democratic lot are these aristocratic Spaniards! How can one but cease to take anxious thought for the morrow in the present delight of the seeing eye and the hearing ear! It is all so gay, the running fire of banter so good natured. Happiness is everywhere.

Of course, no woman should, and therefore every woman does, walk the length of this narrow thoroughfare. She is always looking her best, be assured, conscious that all the way down the street she is being criticized by connoisseurs, and realizing that this audience are implicit believers in the old Spanish proverb that a well-formed woman is far superior to one merely well informed.

Not one, not even a girl often, but wears a flower—a yellow rose, a deep carnation, or dark violets that fade into the shadows of her hair. Unconcernedly they saunter along the promenade, with never a start when some man, staring straight into their eyes, extravagantly exclaims, "How lovely you are! Your eyes burn into my soul!" And those often glorious, downcast eyes, that know so well how to war on men's hearts, will suddenly open and flash a dazzling glance like a slow caress. But it means absolutely nothing—beyond, perhaps, appreciation of the flattering remark.

Here come three daughters and a mother. The proverb says that this means there are four devils for the father; and one of them looks her part, a magnetic young rascal with sun laughter bubbling in her big, luminous eyes. Remarkably tiny feet she has, too, which our table companion notes with the laughing remark, "You should sell those eyes and buy some feet." Is she insulted? Not a whit; merely a slight flush of pleasure damasks her cheeks.

And very noticeable are the little feet even of the humbler class; and such lovely hands of tapering fingers and perfect shape. Something of well-bred heritage there. These mediums of all our actions must be a symbol of the inner self, and the owners of such delicate hands cannot but be aristocrats by nature.

This playground street is one long line of cafés and clubs, whose habitués now sit out of doors. The white-napkined tables within are unoccupied, the rainbow-tinted pastry, temptingly displayed in files of glass cases, untouched; but in the late evening the inner rooms will be packed to suffocation. Then, to the humming and strumming of guitars, young girls will sway in dances of naughty innocence or frank devil-may-care indecency. Spanish men delight in violent sensations, and one of their passions is dancing.

Apparently every city has its gathering place for the bullfighting fraternity—usually named after some local celebrity. Just across the narrow way, with wicker chairs and tables set out on the sidewalk, is the famous Guerrita Club, beloved by all *aficionados*. Here Guerrita reigns supreme, one of the few remaining matadors who still cling to old traditions, and the only one, so far seen outside a bull ring, dressed in traditional costume—the frilled shirt with diamond studs, the collar clasped by gold fastenings, trousers exceedingly tight about the hips, and a short coat resembling an Eton jacket. He is a dignified old fellow, and we "get as many eyes" as the famous matador himself, when he courteously escorts us through the rooms of his club. The ceilings are painted with the brand marks of Spain's most celebrated herds, and every inch of the walls is covered with the heads of bulls—every one with a record for special bravery, every one killed by Guerrita himself. He rather vainly shows us the engrossed scroll record of his killings—2,338 in all. He has now retired, a rich man, credited with ten million pesetas and resultantly honored by his townspeople. We left him with the 'ternal cigarette in his mouth, and he is probably smoking still—if not on earth, somewhere.

Something of a relief it is to turn into the quiet of the beautiful palace of the Marques de Vivani, a livable, homely place, which, from the tablet proudly and conspicuously placed near the entrance door, only last year was honored by a visit from His Majesty the King—a luxury that must have been of equal relief to the King, after the strict etiquette and gorgeous splendor of royal surroundings. To be sure, the rooms are hung with priceless tapestries, and from the vaulted ceilings of age-blackened oak hang curiously wrought chandeliers for which an antiquarian would sell his soul. But these pale before the glory of the patio rooms, with their open, white-pillared galleries that transform this palace into a house of flowers, a garden of sweet-scented jasmine and tumbling wisteria, with century-old clipped box winding in maze. Even the protecting walls are embroidered with roses of pale yellow, blossoms of vivid red, and spreading orange trees. Here is to be found the peace of contentment. Undisturbed, the birds may trill their vesper songs. It is so quiet. From the overlooking balcony we study the cloud shadows in the pools beneath and dreamily watch the river of Time flow by.

April 7

Rough cobble-paved streets, the first, so says history, ever paved in Europe—and apparently never repaved—lead to the city's exit gate. Near by exultantly rises a Triunfo, in honor of the archangel Raphael. According to documents still extant, the archangel appeared before the good Bishop of Cordova, swearing by Jesus Christ Crucified that he was Raphael, the angel under whose protection God had placed the city.

141

Be that as it may, there stands the carved likeness of the archangel, before which every passer-by stops for a brief moment to make the sign of the cross and mumble a hurried plea for intercession. Just in front, the old Moorish bridge of Calahorra straggles across the tawny Guadalquivir with graceful arches. Over it flows back and forth a ceaseless stream of heavily laden donkeys, in charge of human bundles of picturesque rags, who urge forward the slow-plodding beasts with sharp, guttural cries of *"¡Arre burro!"* These burros of Spain, wise with a great wisdom, never seem to revolt, never appear frightened, whatever the provocation; it would only entail unnecessary exertion and useless effort, and their one thought in life is how to do the least work with the least fatigue.

In their wake we cross the dull swirl of yellowed water whose rapids have piled up shoals of ocher sand, offering secure anchorage for the Arab water mills. These mills, painted by the sun of centuries the colors of Mother Earth, still grind the city's corn. Then, out through the Campo de la Verdad we pass the "field where the truth shall be known," as Henry, the bastard brother of Pedro the Cruel, called it when he sallied forth from the city to meet the besieging enemy, destroying as he went the key arch of the bridge so there should be no way of retreat for cowards. Even from this distance we can hear the deep sound of the *Mezquita* bell as it sonorously, rhythmically tolls the hour, responded to by every belfry in the city, their mingled music spreading over the plain until it loses itself in the distance and dies away sweetly.

These plains undulate like a sea of immense waves, taking on, the farther we go, hotter and hotter tones. There is a note of the eternal South in the endless succession of olive trees that twist themselves into agonizing, grotesque shapes like bewitched evil spirits, giving, however, as all ugly things sometimes do, a hint of beauty when the sun snatches from their grayish leaves flashes of silver.

The sun is peculiarly hot and caressing as we near Ecija, *la Ciudad de Sol,*—whose coat of arms is a red disk shooting forth fiery rays,—a sun that paints this drowsing city with brilliant colors that vie with the gaudy-striped awnings covering street and patio, fighting the heat.

Quite outside the beaten path, Ecija remains distinctly Moorish. As one writer relates, it so far preserves the old style as to have no windows within reach of the ground, forcing lovers to take advantage of the slit at the bottom of the house door. There, in the still hours of the night, they stretch out at full length, on opposite sides of this unfriendly barrier, to whisper amorous words of safeguarded passion. We saw none of this, however, being in Ecija at the siesta hour, when all Spain sleeps—even lovers.

But no, the church never sleeps. A pure white sanctuary, rich with gilded woodwork, is filled with sweet-faced nuns, kneeling in prayer; and on entering the convent patio, a place of shady trees and chattering birds, we see white-robed sisters heaping baskets with sprays of jasmine, which they reverently place at the feet of the Christ on the garden altar.

After beaming-faced Ecija, the arid plains seem more than ever melancholy, brightened only when some cheery peasant ambles by on a donkey, his wife clinging behind, with her arms about his waist; or when the roof-peak of one of the miserable hovels of thatch, like the storied home of Robinson Crusoe, serves as a nest for storks, their white wings and red legs against a blue sky making a picture not unlike some Japanese screen.

The gray landscape succeeds only too well in

attuning our mood to the next town of Carmona, with its tombs of grinning skulls. To the flicker of wax tapers we wander through the dark, damp excavations, exploring the subterranean graves of a forgotten race. An appetizing feast for a well-trained archeologist, but we have traveled too far along the road of life to take kindly to these signs of death, and we gladly escape into the sunshine, hurrying toward the city of light and love. Orchards of oranges soon come into view, where, as the Arab poets express it, "globes of oriental topaz glitter among the emerald branches." In another moment we reach the little chapel that marks the city's boundary—the same distance from Seville cathedral as Christ was supposed to have walked on his way to be crucified.

7

Seville, the Paradox of Spain

April 8

We have arrived on the eve of Palm Sunday, *Domingo de Ramos,* spring's beautiful feast day, when the earth is awake with flowers that sing hosannas to Christ, meek and lowly. The day that saw a "very great multitude cut down branches from the trees and strew them in the way, crying, Hosanna in the highest, blessed be he that cometh in the name of the Lord."

And in the morning, as from the Moorish towers the Christian bells rang joyously their gladsome notes, a "very great multitude" wended its way to the cathedral for the blessing of symbolic palms.

Within this holy place is the gloom of stupendous masses, a background of darkness in which, at first, we can see nothing; then gradually great columns of soaring magnificence that rise with confident pride detach themselves from the obscurity. Windows radiant with old stained glass reveal themselves, and we become conscious of a poetic splendor that makes us slaves to emotion. For we are reading a page of reverent art idealized by the poetry of heaven.

The organ tide that floods the church carries us to the high altar. There candles glisten against a purple-black veil, like stars. In the glimmering darkness we feel the presence of countless black-robed figures, whose mantilla-covered faces are devoutly lowered as the mystic drama slowly unfolds. Joyous strains from invisible instruments flood the aisles, a harmony of sound that mingles with the chanting of the priests as they solemnly bless palm and olive branches. The music ceases. There is a rustle of many feet, and a procession forms. The sacristan, yellow-wigged and powdered, bearing a silver staff, leads the way. Behind the cross, carried between lighted candles, comes the archbishop, holding his golden crosier. He is followed by bishops with mitered heads, canons in gorgeous violet vestments heavily embroidered in gold, acolytes with incense burners, filling the church with rich perfume, and half a hundred other dignitaries of the church, with all the gorgeous pomp of Rome. In every hand trembles a palm branch, waving and swaying in lovely symbolization of Christ's entry into the holy city. The eye follows the triumphant procession in its march around the church, now in deep shadows, now emerging into the light, seeing nothing but palms, always palms, among whose drooping leaves floats the smoke of incense, its mystic breath seeming to send a shiver like a lightning flash along the uplifted boughs. The flickering lights reapproach the heart of the cathedral. The jubilant songs of that other procession that paid homage to the Son of God ten thousand years ago die away, and the passion of our Lord is intoned.

A young priest, pale-faced and emaciated, comes forward to one pulpit; another, red-faced and sturdy, takes the center, while to the left goes a third, tall and beautiful of face, with tender mouth of sentiment, fit to repeat the words uttered by our Lord. The narrative is recitative, starting with sonorous phrases to which the organ's vox humana, exquisitely sweet, responds in music of minor melody; then is heard a firm, clear voice in which sadness strongly dominates: "He that dippeth his hand with me into the dish shall betray me. Woe unto that man, it were better for him had he never been born." A piercing cry, a falsetto tenor rends the air, a note so acute that it reaches the ceiling, shivering back in defiant utterance. Judas that

betrayed him is saying, "Is it I, Rabbi?" And
the sweet, sad voice responds, "Thou hast said
it." Stringed instruments wail out melodious
cries for mercy and invocations for pardon,
growing louder and louder each moment.
As this strange, passionate music sweeps through
the cathedral, the silent worshipers kneel in the
grasp of desolation.

Another morning, another drama. "The veil
of the temple is to be rent in twain"—that great,
white curtain that hangs in front of the high
altar, dropping from the airy heights of the
groined ceiling straight down to the mosaicked
floor. It is another sacred and solemn ceremony,
enacted between the choir and the altar, where,
within the narrow, railed lane, pass and repass
priests and acolytes, censers and choristers. Soft
gentle faces, delicate, spiritual faces, dark, hawk-
like faces; men lean and men of much fatness,
for most of whom life is at an end, in bitter contrast to the mischievous-faced altar boys, whose
life has barely begun.

From the deep-toned organ comes a burst of
sound like unto an earthquake. Up to the
dimmed altar majestically sweep bishops and
canons, gorgeous in their robes. A monotonous

rhythmic clink of censer chains, and the air is blue with incense smoke. Gradually follows a thick, black pall, the darkness of Golgotha, and from out this comes a voice saying, "It was almost the sixth hour, and there was darkness over all the earth, and the veil of the temple was rent in twain." A loud thunderclap shatters the silence, wooden hammers beat a dreary tattoo, groans issue from recessed shadows, and the white veil falls apart, torn from top to bottom by invisible hands, snatched into gloomy space before the eye can follow.

Again the scene changes. It is the first darkness of night, and the great building, usually so tenebrous, is aflame with waves of light, the lacy ceiling sparkles with electric stars. One of the great cathedrals of the world becomes to-night a house of music; the gold-screened Capilla Mayor, its high altar stripped of sacred ornament, is the stage. Within its rails sits a great chorus and an orchestra with quaint, old-world instruments. Without, is waiting an audience of thousands, many thousands, twenty-five in all. We are to hear the wondrous "Miserere" of Eslava—Miguel Eslava, who not only sang in the choir and played the violin, but became the cathedral's celebrated maestro organist. It was while dreaming at the keys of this great organ that he caught the divine harmonies of his "Miserere."

But the time is not yet, for centered above the somber *coro* is a triangular candlestick bearing fifteen candles, seven on either side and one at the top—four being still alight. The low chanting of priests is heard. They are singing the pitiful psalm lament, commemorating the suffering and death of Christ. A despairing cry trembles over the scarlet-hung choir: "And they gave me gall for my food, and in my thirst vinegar to drink. Save me, O God, for the waters have come even unto my soul!" In the following silence a candle is extinguished, and one by one each of the symbols of the Apostles is snuffed out, until the taper at the top alone remains alight, in memory of the unquenchable light of the world. With due solemnity, this is taken down and carried behind the altar, the priest conductor waves his baton, and a marvelous fugue begins, a mellow baritone and a magnificent bass swelling into one glorious harmony; youthful voices of boy sopranos, rising and falling to the rhythm, approach almost undreamed register, fading away as the organ gives forth its stored wealth. The anthem ceases as suddenly as it begins. There is a last joyous burst, strangely cheerful for a miserere, and tender passages like love serenades, so touching the heart with their divine glory that scarcely a sound is heard as the vast throng goes into the open, where the sky, transplendent with countless stars, is an echo of the heavenly music.

April 13

It is the Thursday before Easter, the day which commemorates the last supper of Christ with his fellows, when our world is supposed to be clothed in the symbolic garments of mourning and solemnity. Yet the face of Seville lights up with a smile peculiarly feminine. A smile of anticipation, perhaps, for Maundy Thursday seems to be dedicated to Spanish women, usually so orientally guarded, but for whom to-day the artificial bonds of restraint are temporarily loosened.

The city is strangely quiet. Until Saturday no carriage or wheeled traffic will be allowed on the streets; automobiles lie unused in their garages, horses are tied in their stalls, street cars are locked behind heavy doors, and even the humble bicycle is stored away. To ears accustomed to the deafening rumble of wheels, the whisper of many footsteps and the low voices of men and women passing in the streets seem like the dream noises of a city asleep.

Yet every thoroughfare is thronged, filled with women. Jeweled and flower bedecked, wearing that survival of the Mohammedan veil—the white mantilla—in honor of the blessed Christian sacrament, they go from church to church and kneel in graceful groups around the exposed Host. After a prayer or two and a touch of the lips to crossed thumb and first finger, they look about them to see who is there also. It is a sort of trysting day when the social world meets together. Ample-bosomed mamas, still engaging, despite amplitude of figure, in their becoming gowns of black,—which Spain long ago taught was the secret of dress success for dark women,—will cheer their hearts with neighborly gossip; while their jetty-lashed, youthful daughters make full use of that faithful ally of the coquetry of Spanish women—the mantilla, which knows no age, is ever young and always becoming. Veiled in this bit of white lace which falls simply over a high comb, a woman would have to be as ugly as the seven deadly sins not to be bewitching. It is the symbol of one who conceals her charms; behind it she may hide or come out into the open, like the closing or shutting of a door.

On arrival at their own parish church, the women remain most of the day seated at tables between lighted candles, an open tray before them, wheedling from adoring satellites money with which to buy jewels for their favorite Virgin. The heavy leather hangings curtaining the entrance are forever aswing to the passing of a ceaseless stream of old gallants and young beaux suddenly seized with religious fervor. Their devotion, however, is paid only to the "Madonnas of the Tables," who, from the dusk of their cloudy mantillas send forth such dangerous lightnings of appeal as to be perfectly irresistible. For many a young girl Maundy Thursday holds the golden hour of her life, and when she leaves the sacred edifice, it is to her more than ever hallowed.

No man counts the hours when playing along such paths of feminine beauty as Maundy Thursday opens, but evening seems to creep in long before its allotted time, and with the falling shadows of night comes another change of mood, one that is heavy with the melancholy of the dying day, settling upon the sensitized soul a weight of impending grief. The hour has struck for those sorrowful processions of religion so intimately woven into the life of Seville.

There is a distant fanfare of trumpets. Out from the narrow, sinuous Calle de las Sierpes (Street of the Serpents) into the full glare of the electric-lighted square rides a troop of resplendent buglers, sounding a plaintive, musical wail, a quavering lament that reaches the highest pitch, lingers a moment, and is gone. Then in swaying march appear weird, ghostly figures dressed in long, shapeless tunics of white, and wearing a high, sharp-peaked hood that falls over the shoulders and far down the front, leaving only eyes visible. The leaders carry in white-gloved hands silver staffs of authority; others hold aloft banners of black velvet on which glitter in gold the Roman letters S. P. Q., in remembrance of the part played in this drama by the Roman Governor, Pontius Pilate; the remainder bear long, heavy candles which they place at rest on the ground as they halt in the center of the square, facing one another.

A funeral dirge breaks the hushed silence, and a group of acolytes approach, some with antique silver crosses, others with long silver poles that end in smoking torches; choristers and church dignitaries in vestments rich with golden embroidery follow, and then a huge catafalque, twinkling with gilded candelabra and wrapped in a cloud of incense. It bears a life-size figure of Christ, staggering beneath an enormous cross of tortoise shell and gold. The face is ghastly with pain, a terrifying, realistic illusion of such intense suffering that the religious emotion of the crowd is contagious. Slowly and laboriously it moves, borne on the shoulders of wearied men, who are concealed from sight by heavy hangings. On reaching the crimson-draped *Ayuntamiento* (town hall), the *paso* gives a half turn so that the image may face the high officials, whom it seems to salute, tipping slightly as the bearers bend their knees.

Drums beat more loudly, trumpets continue their gloomy blast, and the procession proceeds. But soon the carriers must rest, and to the sharp tap of the leader's metal staff the saintly platform halts. There is a perfect Babel of sound. High above the chants of priests can be heard the cry of *"¡Agua, quien quiere agua!"* mingled with the voice of the cake vender advertising his wares, *"¡Dulces! ¡Dulces!"* Profiting by a moment of silence, some man standing directly in

front of the figure of Christ will launch a *saeta*
—an arrow of song, an improvisation of almost
startling fierceness and passionate sadness, his
voice rising and falling in heart-rending notes,
the song ending with a light trill palpitating
with joy.

A hammer strikes the metal edge of the platform with a note of warning. The pause has
been long enough. At a word of command, the
figure is raised again, and the feet of the
hidden porters toil farther along their *Via
Crucis*.

More hooded figures are approaching. They
hold in gloved hands long trumpets, which sound
a shrill blast. Then, "Hush, she comes!" is
heard in awe-stricken whispers, and under a
canopy of brocade, upheld by silver poles, there
slowly appears a statue of the Virgin, bright with
the brightness of a hundred candles. She is arrayed in black velvet embroidered with palm
leaves of gold, and a long train trails far behind.
From throat to waist she is covered with superb
jewels, even the tears raining down her cheeks
are pearls, and in the glare of the candles dazzling rays flash from a huge diamond that drops
low on her forehead. A shower of flowers falls
from the balconies overhead, and eager faces

look down upon eager faces looking up. The deluge of petals soon covers the street with a mantle of many shades. The air is hot with pungent incense and noisy with the roll of drums and solemn chants.

One after another they come,—Our Lady of Solitude; the Descent from the Cross; Piety; Calvary; Conception; the Expiation,—an endless procession, each in charge of its own special fraternity, hooded in purple, blue, magenta, or black.

Slowly they are borne into the cathedral, whose doors stand open all through the night. They wind their way through the somber aisles, whose darkness even the smoking torches and countless candles fail to dissipate, and then out again into the calm beauty of this Southern night.

Within the church the people walk to and fro with the easy familiarity of the street. A whole family lies prostrate on the floor, oblivious to the noise, in wearied sleep. Mothers care for babies as only mothers can. Gentle nuns are jostled by sulky, angry-eyed gypsies. Beggars in tatters crowd the rich. A confused mass it is, of standing, kneeling, crouching figures in unconscious artistic pose.

It is already nearing the second hour of the morning when we reach the Plaza de San Lorenzo, where in darkness and silence a great multitude anxiously waits. A shiver of emotion and reverential fear runs through the gathered throng on hearing the church clock begin to strike the hour. One—two—. With the second vibrating stroke still hovering in the air, the great doors of San Lorenzo swing open, flooding the square with light as though the hand of God had unbolted the doors of shining heaven. The church within seems afire—one compact mass of flaming candles, which, two by two, slowly detach themselves. Two by two, mysterious black-hooded figures step out into the open, without a word, obliged to keep silence by the oath of brotherhood. They push a lane through the seething crowd, holding their candles aslant, that the hot grease may sear the sacrilegious flesh of any loiterers in the path of the approaching *paso*. *Nuestro Señor del Gran Poder* (Our Lord of Great Power) advances, standing on a silver platform at the four corners of which are grouped adoring angels. The genius of the sculptor Montanes has immortalized the great Martyr with a tragical bloodstained figure, stumbling over the stones, borne

159

down by the weight of his cross; his face stained by the sweat of death.

In a glorious stream of light the *paso* moves down the path hewn through the mob by the black stream of Nazarenes. Except for murmurs of praise, wonder, and low petitions, "O Lord of Power, remember us, remember us!" the quiet is unbroken, as though fearing to profane the mystery of this journey of Christ.

How startlingly different is the wild and deafening acclaim that greets the idol Virgin of the populace, *María de la Esperanza,* Macarena's Lady of Hope. She little resembles other conceptions of the Virgin in the days approaching the passion, but rather a Mary in sublime youth, embodying a pretty woman of the people, with the full, supple curves of the Sevillian figure. Her head is carried slightly bent as if seeking with her glance all helpless creatures, forcing even those without faith to love and worship her. In her pilgrimage through the streets the air rings with shouts of admiration, and lovesongs innumerable are hurled after this Mary of Bethlehem.

No one knows the master carver who brought her into being. Tradition says that one day two young men, announcing themselves as sculptors, offered to chisel a figure, if given a closed room and food for three days. The three days passed, and the door remained closed until forced, when the food was found untouched, the sculptors vanished, leaving behind this Virgin of Macarena—and another miracle passed into religious history.

The beat of drums heralds the dawn, and in the Calle del Popolo, before the city jail, is Macarena's jealous rival, the Virgin from Triana, the gypsy quarter, paying her annual visit of consolation to the women prisoners. An old hag, one of the derelicts on life's stream, stretches out her hand between the bars touching the figure of the Virgin, and from between her cracked lips issues a strange wail, like the cry of a soul heavy with agony. It is a *saeta,* a love-song to the dusky-eyed Virgin:

> The eyes of my dark Virgin
> Are like the wounds I bear;
> Great as my desolation,
> Black as my despair.

Behold, the west is filled with the radiance of pure gold! The sun shines and the birds sing! How can such things be?

No sooner has the religious fervor of *Semana Santa* (Holy Week) exhausted itself, than the merry *Feria* opens its doors. Then Seville becomes as gay as a young beauty on the threshold of her début, beaming with a joy in which you sense a caressing atmosphere, full of the sap of life. Religion and love are the only two matters of serious import to Sevillian women.

Overnight the Calle San Fernando and the adjoining *paseos* have been strung with fanciful aërial lights; Japanese lanterns festoon the roadsides, red and yellow bunting waves from tall poles, and firefly lamps twinkle in the shrubbery of the gardens.

Out in the open, long avenues of *casetas* (small houses) have sprung into being; houses that are open to the street, where there is no privacy, no doors or windows, no front at all to hinder you from looking within. Completely furnished, they resemble the doll houses of our childhood. Here is the playground of fashion.

But in the field of the Prado de San Sebastián is a great encampment of a thousand animals— sheep, horses, mules, and pigs, jumbled together in a confusion dirtily picturesque. Here is the actual *Feria*—a country fair of merry-go-rounds, circus tents, and side shows, open-air shops, venders of toys and edibles. There are pans of dried crabs and *buñuelos,* a sort of doughnut, fresh from their fiery bath of thick, black oil, that gives, not only local color, but a decided local odor. Gypsies in crimson shawls, with coarse, black hair like the tail of a horse, pluck at our sleeves to entice us into their tents of fortune. Serious-faced peasants in festive dress, and, though the day is warm, with the inevitable *manta*—striped blanket folded over the shoulder —hurry to and fro. Horses dash back and forth, now at a walk, now at full gallop, showing off their best points. Donkeys are ridden up and down in front of possible purchasers. One mischievous little burro tosses his master into the black mud of the miry roadway, and the discomfited seller tries to laugh as he shouts at the offending donkey, *"¡Y pensar que tengo que hablar bien de ti!"* (Only to think that I have to speak well of you!) Pandemonium reigns; but the haggling, chaffing banter is good-natured and in holiday humor.

In the late afternoon, vehicles six abreast trail along the broad *paseo,* the plebeian and the aristocrat of the carriage world rubbing shoulders. There are splendid landaus drawn by magnificent horses, with drivers resplendent in rosettes and gold braid, and shabby victorias with shabbier coachmen. Spanking four-in-hands of swift, black mules go side by side with spiked teams, tandems, and strange conveyances whose horses are covered with chenille-fringed leather trimmed with great pompons of green, red, and yellow. For the most part these are graced by woman,—woman at her best,—dressed in her best, in her most becoming gown, with her most exquisite jewels, her face framed in the mystery of the mantilla held in place with fragrant flowers, leaning against a background of splashing color painted by the gorgeous Manila shawls spread over the carriage seat. All the beauty of Seville is on parade, and the most beautiful are applauded as they pass, with cries of *"¡Viva la Gracia!"* (Long life to Beauty!) to which Beauty responds with a wave from the supplemental fingers of her ever present fan.

After nightfall some of these same picturesque shawls will be girded tight to flexible figures, in preparation for the *seguidilla*. In any of the open-air ballrooms of the *casetas* you may chance upon two girls, one in a gown of white, with a flaming rose at the waist, hair drawn into a low knot, black against the white of her neck, seated at a piano; the other, in the foreground, is sheathed in the oriental shawl, black and gold with stabs of red and yellow. She is passing her fingers between the silken cords of the castanets, which begin to click almost as naturally as the fingers snap. The cords of a guitar will be swept with that curious ringing touch of Andalusian Spain, and, seized by the spirit of the dance, the inamorata clicks her heels against the hardwood floor, and her body springs to life as vivid as a flower. With arms raised, lips slightly parted, eyelashes lowered, she dances, lost in the music, unconscious of the passing throng, who in eager-watching crowds mass around the open enclosure, so interested that half-smoked cigarettes fall to the ground. At length, in the lifting drift of the blue smoke, the dance comes to an end.

Only around the exclusive club of Labradores are screening curtains hung. Behind this shelter Royalty, with the fairest and most patrician of Sevillian society, make merry. Possibly we fail to find even there the supreme beauty heralded with such extravagant praise. But there are many, many bewitching faces, and such lovely heads of hair, in which all this week appear the famous *claveles*—Seville's coral-colored carnations. Over their black locks are spun spider webs of white transparent lace—the ever graceful mantilla, and from their ears dangle earrings of jade, filigree gold, or coral, that glow against the cheeks olived by the African sun.

But there are blond heads too, and blue eyes, inherited from the Visigoths and the time of Alauf and Theodoric, whose long-forgotten peccadillos have enriched the English language with the term "blue blood"—*sangre azul;* for side by side with Spain's prevalent brunette, the blue-blood veins show very clearly beneath the blond skins. These fair-haired ones dress in white, with black mantillas and roses of a dying tint thrust among their sunny curls. All, blond and brunette alike, are wrapped in shawls, whose embroidered flowers give the illusion of huge bouquets.

To-night señora mamas, recalling their own youthful follies, remain far in the background, where they converse together in whispers, with the air of so many conspirators, apparently taking no heed of the audacious freedom of this *Feria* week.

Most of the evening modern dancing claims this cosmopolitan floor, but now and again the rhythmic beat of castanets and the tinkle of

tambourines replaces the music of the orchestra.
Then one of those light-hearted Sevillianas with
its subtle grace puts to shame the clumsy ca-
prices of present fashion.

It is almost morning, and out of doors we find
the curtain of heaven has closed around the stars,
the street fairy lights are extinguished, the Prado
is asleep, plunged in deep darkness, where wander shadows blacker than the night, guarding
their animal charges. Along the field roads are
faint glimmers of dying fires that cast dancing
silhouettes across the ragged tents in which sleep
the Bohemian riffraff of the fair. Then all
things melt into an eternity of darkness.

April 18

So far we have used only religious blacks and
carnival reds to paint the picture, but many other
colors must be brushed in before you distinguish
even the hazy outline of reality that forms this
beautiful "paradox of Spain."

In the immediate foreground should come
that glorious sentinel tower climbing skyward
beside the cathedral, the Giralda, capped by a
dome on which stands a bronze figure of "Faith."
Every shift of the fickle wind this beautiful

167

statue responds to, giving the name *Giraldillo* (vane) to the tower. And in the religious storms of centuries, Faith has veered from the pagan cult of Venus to Allah—and now to God. But the tower is the same, except for the belfry, the Christian substitute for the voice of the muezzin calling to prayers as the sun tints the sky at its setting *"La-ilaha-illa-'llahu."* It still speaks in the poesy of the Orient, with its network of arabesque sunken panels and its windows of graceful ajiminez, and from the streets below come stealing up faint echoes of those same barbaric chants sung when the caliphs held sway.

Let us mount the inclined plane that leads to the top. We shall have to go together, for to go alone is prohibited by law—so many lonely souls chose Giralda as the road to reach heaven before God called them.

When we arrive at the upper gallery, where the six bells hang in open arches, it is to find them loudly clamoring a call to prayers; even La Gorda, the fat, is adding her deep voice to the deafening din. Around and around she swings in complete circles, winding about her axle the rope which forces her to speak. With every turn she drags from the ringer's hands a certain well-marked section of hempen cable, until

THE GIRALDA, SEVILLE.

AIRPLANE VIEW OF SEVILLE, THE CATHEDRAL IN THE CENTER.

only five pieces are left, then two, then one. Now the man runs swiftly up the steps notched in the stone wall, throws himself out into the open, and with his weight pulls the bell in the opposite direction, unwinding the rope. If not timed accurately, another bell ringer would probably have gone where sometime all good little bell ringers have to go.

Far, far below, the flying buttresses of the cathedral look not unlike the skeleton ribs of some prehistoric fossil bleaching under the torrid sun. So high are we that the view is not unlike that from some soaring aëroplane, forcing Seville to open wide every gate of beauty. Immediately beneath is the Court of Oranges, the *Patio de los Naranjos.* Through the Puerta del Perdón, open in pardon to every wickedness except heresy, float the diminutive shadows of sin-stricken penitents, who stop to kneel on the bare stones in front of the modern shrine before entering the cathedral. In the corner of the court, hanging above the doorway of Lagarto, can dimly be seen the huge stuffed crocodile, sent long years ago by a sultan of Egypt as a present, when asking the hand of Seville's most beautiful princess in marriage. The marriage was declined, but the present was kept, in memorial of

169

this "consuming" passion, finding its way at length to the cathedral, which, like all churches in early days, was a museum for the beautiful and curious alike.

From our aërial post of observation we can easily follow the broad path of the Guadalquivir —the Wod-el-Kebir of the Arabs—until it loses itself in the vague distance, its storied waters overflowing with historic memories of the days when Spanish galleons sought the treasures of the Incas. Every ship sailing for the New World left from here; all the returning "Golden Fleets," laden with spoils came back here, pouring their treasures into the Moorish tower still standing on the brim of the river, heaping it high with dishes of gold, crowns of gold, spears and daggers with hilts of gold—nothing but gold—until it baptized the tower for all times with the name "Torre de Oro."

Directly in front of us the brown-visaged Alcázar shows against the azure sky, each of its stones guarding some romantic story. Here, as Omar says, "Sultan after sultan abode his destined hour and went his way."

It is another of those marvelous Moorish palaces, whose walls are covered with stucco tapestry—a needlework in plaster, interwoven

170

with the wildest profusion of filmy ornament, making a petrified veil of lace. A fairy palace, too bright and too gaudy perhaps for those who love the more mysterious charm of the Alhambra of Granada, whose decorations it borrows, but still a dazzling jewel of which Spain is justly proud.

The long-past days have seen many a haunting presence pass through these courts and patios, but even the pious memory of Isabella the Catholic, by whose orders all rogues were obliged to leave Seville,—greatly depopulating the city, as the chronicles quaintly relate,—is unable to drive away the dominant figures of Pedro the Cruel and María de Padilla.

Pedro the Cruel was to Seville what Harun al Raschid was to Bagdad, though he found no Scheherezade to tell his story. In imitation of his Bagdad prototype, Pedro was wont to wander through the streets in disguise, and in one of his midnight rambles, masked and closely muffled, he was walking through a dark alley leading from the Plaza de San Isidoro, when a man knocked against him. Pedro, furious, drew his sword and killed the man in a desperate duel, forgetting in his blind rage that he himself had made a law forbidding all fighting in the streets upon pain of death. What should he do? His twisted sense of humor suggested an idea. He would punish the Alcaide, the mayor of the city, for not having guards about so that such a thing could not happen. When, the following morning, the dead body was discovered, he warned the Alcaide that if the criminal were not found, he should hang in his place. Luckily for the Alcaide, an old woman had heard the clatter of swords during the fight and had lighted a candle to look out. The light had fallen full upon the King, whose mask had slipped, and she notified the Alcaide. Fortunately for him he possessed imagination. Making a dummy of the king, he dressed it in royal robes and hung it on a gallows raised in the central square. In remembrance, Seville named the street where the old woman looked out of the window the Calle del Rey Don Pedro, and so it is known to this very day.

More Moorish than Christian, a monster of historic cruelty, voluptuous and unscrupulous, was Pedro. The only unsullied flower not choked by the rank weeds of a long life of vice was his passionate adoring love for María de Padilla, a dark vision of beauty, according to historians, who reigned until death as uncrowned queen, a queen of love—and there is none higher.

What gardens of enchantment are within the Alcázar, so full of mystery, with the sound of invisible fountains that are never silenced! Stately terraces lead down into quiet patios, where the walls are orange lined, the golden fruit hanging temptingly within reach of every hand. All the paths are hedged with banks of myrtle, whose fragrance mingles with the sweet scent of the magnolias waving above a tangled mass of roses, so peaceful and undisturbed that within the birds have built their nests.

The beauties that lurk here in every shadow have been dragged into light by those spiritual, clever Sevillianos, the Quintero brothers, who may be seen almost any day walking up and down these rose-bordered paths, creating in repartee, with much gesticulation, the lively dialogue which is the fascination of their work. No one ever knows what part one writes or what part the other. Many of their plays have been written right here, presenting Andalusian types, scenes, and events that make us acquainted, as no others, with this land of the Blessed Virgin. Always sweet and clean, they depict Seville as Seville imagines herself to be,—though a friend writing from Seville says she once accused Serafin Quintero of not being true to fact. He appeared as though physically hurt, she goes on to say, answering after a moment's hesitation, "It is true, true as we see it." And I had to confess that it might be so, that genius might purify fact.

These two brothers represent the perfume of Andalusia translated into intellectual terms. Of all writers of light comedy they are without doubt the cleverest—frothy, foolish, tender, childish fun; nothing unkind, never anything suggestive, always subtle and refined. Their success rests upon the humorous rather than the dramatic. Since 1886, when, as subofficials in the dry, red-taped Ministry of Finance, they wrote their first play, they have produced over one hundred and thirty, without scoring one real failure. Quite simple, they assert, nothing but resetting the thousand and one jeweled quips and quirks daily overhead in this land where playing with words and phrases is almost a cult, giving them a clever twist that turns the usual into the witty unusual.

This playing with words is as habitual with the lower as with the higher classes. Well do I remember our Sevillian coachman who appeared one morning at the hotel, driving a horse so weak with age that he fairly tottered on his feeble legs. On seeing him, we laughingly said, *"Debe ir á la Plaza de Toros"* (He ought to go to the bull ring). *"No,"* was the quick response *"¿No ve usted que es un bailador?"* (No, don't you see that he is a dancer?)

Among the Quinteros' best-known plays is *El Genio Alegre* (The Spirit of Happiness). The action develops in the little town of *Alminar de la Reina,* a fictitious name which, like *Puebla de las Mujeres, Arenales del Rio,* and a dozen others, the brothers Quintero have lastingly placed on the map of Spain. The setting is one of those Old World estates where long-drawn-out years are passed after the fashion of the hidalgoes of Spain, amid austere, cloister-like surroundings, in great rooms filled with age-darkened family portraits. A veritable sepulcher for the living. This severe, monotonous life where laughter and merriment was immediately repressed, has driven Julio, the son of the house, to Madrid. His mother, broken-hearted at his long absences, reproaches him when he tries to explain that they look upon life from totally different standpoints.

"For you, Mother, life is a martyrdom; for me it represents pleasure. For you the world is a valley of tears; for me a field of flowers. You must live as if in a dark cloister, while I wish the sun to shine in my face. If life is gay, as I believe, why make it sad? If sad, as you think, is it not more human to enliven it a little?"

Now a girl cousin, Consolation, appears on the scene, charming, full of the joy of happiness, of youth and beauty. Finding the austerity and silence of the house almost unbearable, she resolves to change it, and discovers a more than willing ally in the son, Julio, who believes with her that to enjoy life is to love it, and to love it is a way of adoring God, who gave it to us. They are firmly convinced that a happy nature is the noblest, the least egoistic.

All the faithful old servants respect and conform to the austere habits of the house, all but Lucio, a typical young Andalusian, who is ever astounded when the mistress of the house finds fault with him when he laughs and sings too much; and she is always scolding. "Who has been the telltale, Madame la Marquisa?" he asks, again and again. "The swallows told me," invariably replies the mistress. And as day after day his every fault of song and laughter is whispered to the Marquisa by the swallows, naturally Lucio becomes very resentful of the spiteful birds, and only awaits an opportunity to get even with them. This presents itself when Consolation finally succeeds in transforming the gloomy old house patio into a bright garden of smiling flowers, to the stupefaction of the Marquisa, who unexpectedly enters. Finding her son, Julio, Consolation, and the servant Lucio hard at work, she turns in amazement to Julio for an explanation.

"What does this mean, Julio?"

Julio replies, "Ask Consolation."

"What does this mean, Consolation?"

"Ask Lucio," answers Consolation.

"What is this, Lucio?"

Says Lucio, "Ask the swallows, Ma'm."

At last the good mother, overjoyed that Julio stays for two consecutive days in the old manor, discovers that the real means of keeping him at home is to make home cheerful and happy. She is more than elated when Julio, declaring his love for Consolation, decides never to return to Madrid. Julio tells Consolation that with her the sunshine has entered the house. "You brought it by the hand—or was it in your eyes? But you brought it some way. It entered this house of ours, closed to all light like a sepulcher, and illumined every corner. The doors and windows opened and let in the sweet air of a merry life, that life that was given us, that we should use it worthily, wisely."

It is little to our credit that the work of the Quintero brothers is known to almost every language in the world except English.

The Alcázar with its troubled memories of Don Pedro the Cruel, brings to mind another figure of no small fame in poetry and music, that of Pedro's boon companion, Don Juan de Mañara, the Don Giovanni of Mozart, dreaded by husbands and fathers alike. To no purpose were locks put on patio gates and iron bars over the windows of their fair ones, for Don Juan's creed was that he owed himself to pretty women in general, and the mere fact of having met one did not absolve him from his duty to others. In life he was not the Giovanni of the stage, elegant in velvet and lace, but, living in warlike times, he was soberly dressed, yet with all the dash and bravery that pleases a woman's eye. He lived not far from the Alcázar, in fact very near the house of that other musical hero, the Barber of Seville, the factotum of the town, "whose number is fifteen on the left-hand side" in the Plaza San Thomas, right around the corner from a dimly lighted calle, with projecting balconies, just as we see it in the first scene of the opera.

There actually was a commandant belonging to the order of Calatrava, who, the chronicles insist, was killed by Don Juan when abducting Donna Anna, though legend does not accept the ghostly supper party with the statue of the dead father as guest. Preferred is the story that one night, when wandering through the dark streets, Don Juan met a funeral procession, a long procession of shrouded figures chanting the death dirge and showing all the insignia of some person of high degree. Don Juan spoke to one of the priests, asking whose body it was. "Don Juan de Mañara," was the reply. "Will you not follow and say a prayer for his sinful soul?" Looking into the glass-covered coffin, Don Juan beheld his own face. Spellbound, he followed the spectral throng into the church to listen to his own requiem. Next morning found him insensible on the floor.

After this warning the profligate Don reformed, and to testify to the sincerity of his repentance he founded the hospital known as *La Caridad* (charity), almost within sight of his old home. Cynics assert that when too old to commit more sins, he thus tried to make his peace with the Almighty.

La Caridad is a flowered, peaceful retreat for old men, filmy-eyed and palsied, whose beds of pain and sorrow are made more endurable by the gentle care of white-capped nuns. One of these sisters, in winged headdress, opens the entrance gate in answer to our ring, pointing as she does so to a figure of the Virgin, which bids all who pass to say a prayer—and say it with love, is the final plea—*No me olividas.* There breathes the beautiful spirit of this Hospital de la Caridad, which is "a virtue of the heart and not of the hands." A splendid atonement this, for Don Juan's dissipated youth, despite cynics and scoffers. And so evidently thinks the sister as she lovingly shows the desk at which Don Juan sat, his sword, drawn in many a duel, the spoon and fork used for his monastic fare, and finally his name, first on the engrossed roll of membership in the Brotherhood of Charity.

Not far from the top of this list is the name of Murillo, long a member of the Brotherhood, for whom he painted some of his most celebrated pictures. The most famous, *La Virgen de la Servilleta* (The Virgin of the Napkin), was hastily brushed in for the cook, who had begged for a painted souvenir on the even of Murillo's departure from his cloistered life. Finding all the prepared cloth had been packed away, he brought a napkin to serve as canvas. This picture no longer hangs in the kitchen, but in Seville's museum, among the other Murillo treasures that never fail to touch the heart, depicting, as they do, the soul as well as the body.

Other paintings cover the walls of the peaceful little hospital chapel. And, if the truth must be told, it is one of human nature's paintings that longest holds our eye—a young woman in black mantilla, kneeling before the wooden lattice of the confessional box, whispering her pretty sins to a handsome priest, who eagerly leans far forward so as not to lose the faintest sound. They talk of the love of God, but the picture is one of earthly love, such as may be seen almost any night in almost any Spanish city, before the iron window grilles of some dimly lighted calle.

And what charms lurk in the lilac shadows of those dark, threadlike, winding calles that form the artistic heart of Seville! In the "Jewry" with its intricate turnings and quaint corners, where centuries have stood still, the streets are

so quiet that you catch the whispered words
from the flowered balconies jutting so far out
either side that the rose in one often embraces
the delicate white jasmine of the other. Here
one may walk for hours in the perfume of past
traditions. We find a like charm in the open
plazas, fringed with palms that rustle under the
faintest breeze; or in the delightful gardens
that follow the river in long alleys of sweet-
smelling claveles, where the "topers" and the
snowballs—wine-red and pure white—face one
another in fierce rivalry. We find it even in the
poplar-shaded Alameda, "where honest poverty
and no less honest vice happily gather together."

But perhaps the greatest charm is to be found
within the delightful garden patios, the center
of life in every Sevillian home. Nothing hin-
ders us from looking into the cool, restful court
which, once "the hour of fire" is past, becomes
the family drawing-room, frankly open to all
passers-by. In his famous novel, *La Hermana
San Sulpicio,* Palacio Valdes pictures in one of
them a young girl playing the piano, her
back to the street. "I stopped to listen an instant, and with me a woman of the people, who,
putting her face through the bars, cried, 'Señorita, oh, Señorita!' The young girl turned

around, saying, 'Well, what do you want?' 'Nothing, Señorita! Your figure pleased me so much from behind, I wished to see it from the front.' 'And how am I from the front?' asked the girl, undisturbed. 'Like a rosebud, my heart.' 'Many thanks,' and she turned quietly about and continued playing."

Since the death of Perez Galdós there is no one to dispute the palm with Palacio Valdés, and even that author of the literary historical monument—*The National Episodes*—was Valdés inferior in the creation of character as well as in the love and study of nature. Valdés has perhaps a greater sense of humor than any other contemporary Spanish novelist, and to this Andalusian fund of humor he adds an immense tenderness and mysticism peculiar to the northern provinces, an emotional gift seldom equaled in Spanish literature.

While he has written many novels, Valdés' fame seems to rest on *La Hermana San Sulpicio,* considered a masterpiece by all critics. In it he paints *La Tierra Santissima* with rare fidelity, picturing the sweetly sad poetic soul of Andalusia concealed beneath a fiery exuberance. He describes Sister Saint Sulpicio as a young girl of eighteen, with an oval face of pale brown, velvety eyes of intense black with long eye-lashes, and a seductive grace that showed not alone in her brilliant eyes, not in her mouth or in her slightly retroussé nose, but rather in the illuminating smile which lighted up her entire face. She belonged to the convent of the Heart of Mary in Seville, where the vows of sisterhood were for four years, not becoming perpetual until after twelve years of probation. She was dressed in the white hood and black habit of their novitiates, and from about her neck hung a beautifully carved bronze crucifix. San Juro, the hero of the book, first meets Sister Sulpicio at the Springs of Marmelejo, near Cordova, where they are both stopping for the cure. He naïvely confesses that when, on being intro-duced, he stoops to kiss the metal crucifix hang-ing on her bosom, he does not do so purely from religious impulses, but rather because of the black eyes of the young sister, that smile at him in response to his courtesy.

"I am glad that you smile, even if you smile at me," he said. "Any smile would give pleas-ure from lips so fresh and so pretty."

"Don't you know, Señor, that it is a sin to make compliments to a nun, and much more for her to listen?"

"Then I will confess and be absolved."

"That is not enough: it is necessary to repent and not to sin again."

"But, Sister, that will be difficult."

San Juro of course falls deeply in love, but who has not fallen in love with one of those seductive Spanish nuns, he says! And when in one of their walks around the little village Sister Sulpicio discloses the fact that she does not intend to renew her vows, San Juro tells her of his love, to which she will not listen, being still in orders. But in spite of herself she reveals her pleasure, strengthening San Juro in his resolve to follow her to Seville, where he finally goes, colorfully describing its varied life and its many picturesque types.

Valdés tells this anecdote about an election held in a little town near Seville. One of the candidates for mayor is asked if he won. "I couldn't do otherwise," he replied. "But the secretary who opposed you so fiercely?" "The poor man died." "You don't mean it!" "Yes, just before election. Very curious, too, for when I was here a month ago, talking with the Señor Gobernador, I told him frankly that the secretary was gaining strength and likely to win, unless he, the Gobernador, interfered. Do you know that he told me that he had a premonition that something was going to happen to the secretary before election. Only an omen, to be sure, he said, but he was very much afraid, for whenever he had these warnings something always happened. I forgot all about it until I went back to my village, when a few days later the secretary was found at full length on the road with a hole in his brain. Since then I have always believed in omens."

Interspersed with masterly delineations of character and amusing scenes, the love story of San Juro and Sister Sulpicio gradually unfolds. The Sister, at last freed from the convent, writes San Juro to meet her at the *reja* (barred window), where, in a memorable interview lasting until two o'clock in the morning, they swore eternal love. Gloria—no longer Sister—expressed joy that Saint Elias would not be able to write her down in his notebook, explaining that Saint Elias with pen in hand was carried in the processions of Holy Week, when he inspected all the balconies, making a list of spinsters. As always, the course of true love did not run smoothly, but marriage comes in the last chapter, and Gloria and her husband visit the convent, her home for twelve years, where she is received with slight signs of hostility, natural perhaps from those who believed she had left the "right road." Vexed, Gloria throws her arms about her husband's neck, in order to shock them, kissing him soundly. This so horrifies the nuns that they leave the room, drawing the cords of the curtain behind them, which, as it falls, gives a squeak of scandal.

You should read this book if you would read the heart secrets of Seville, that city of irresistible joy, whose sky, the serene blue of a nun's eyes, brings joy to the city, and the city to the heart of everyone who passes through it. Impossible to be a pessimist in Seville!

Our last recollection of the city is when in the golden dawn trumpets sound from the four sides of the Giralda tower,—the gospel proclamation made to the four winds of heaven,—the sad, clear notes representing the tears of Saint Peter, whom the poets describe as a noble old man weeping for his sin, tearing his white beard as he weeps his bitter tears of grief, sweetened by repentance.

8

Under Andalusian Skies

April 20

In the early morning hours the Paseo de las Delicias (The Walk of Delights), so fittingly named, is entirely deserted. We are alone with its beauties. "The hurrying moments for a while have ceased their journey," and there is the stillness and quiet which alone can bring to the heart a perfect understanding. From beneath the arching trees can be heard the rush or running waters—the tawny Guadalquivir leaping to its deathbed in the distant ocean. Its freshness is married to the fragrance of many roses that spring has showered down in place of rain. They fall in festoons that hedge the road and ramble up the tree trunks in search of the sun. Veritably it is a walk of many delights.

The Paseo leads to the open country and a road bordered with small taverns and eating houses, where gather the *ganaderos* of the bull corrals.

This morning we are watching the fighting bulls being driven in from their pasture lands.

Close to the palisades that separate paddocks from meadow are the fight admirers, eagerly gazing over the green and golden stretch, on the lookout for the animals allotted to the morrow's show. Among the spectators are several ennuied beauties, seeking a new flavor in the spice of danger. Dressed in breeches sashed with crimson silk, short jackets, and broad-brimmed Cordovan hats, with long lances grasped in the right hand, they nervously wait on horseback for a signal from the herders.

Far away we catch sight of fast-moving black specks. Then a loud bellowing is heard and the tinkle of the bell oxen who lead the way. Fighting bulls are accustomed from the day they are born to the noise of these bells and will follow wherever tame bullocks guide. The oncoming sounds send all loiterers scuttling to places of safety, jumping into ditches or behind protecting hedges as the great beasts, moving clumsily but very rapidly, follow closely after the men on horseback at full gallop. In a cloud of dust and with the thunder of heavy rushing feet, they pound down the road, swinging sharply into the open paddock gates for a few more hours of happy grazing, fortunately unable to read the big posters now being placarded on the walls of

the Plaza de Toros, announcing for the morrow
the sale of low-priced bull meat.

Well out in the open are the country homes
of Seville, little white villas hiding behind the
silver-gray of olive trees. They all face the
distant outline of the city, where, massed black
against the sky, shows the great Giralda. Its
beacon tower, thrust high into the upper lights,
transforms the summit into shining yellow topaz,
as the ray children of the sun dance about the
bronze figure of "Faith."

For some distance there prevails the luxury
of the tropics—stately palms, hoary patriarchal
fig trees, houses cloaked in brilliant-colored
flowers, an ardent sun. And then the immense
everlasting plains, carpeted with soft pine and
bristling cactus—the lonely, desolate kingdom
of the royal bulls.

On the river side these plains are bordered by
an ocean of lush grass that forms a veritable animal heaven, where, in Biblical fashion, all bulls
must some day stand before the Judgment Seat,
that the good may be winnowed from the bad—
for every bull on reaching the age of two years
has to submit to a trial that is to decide his life
or death. At the appointed time he is lured by

his bell-ox companions into the presence of the owner-judges. One of the *vaqueros,* mounted on a perfectly trained horse, with *garrocha*—a strong wooden lance twelve feet long, tipped with steel—at rest, rides out to meet him. As he approaches, he bellows the plainsman's arousing cry of *"¡Entra! ¡Entra!"* charging at full speed and driving the steel into the hind quarter of the bull, who topples over on his back, pawing the air. If, nettled by the stinging pain, the bull comes back to the charge a second and a third time, he is declared a *toro bravo* (brave noble) worthy to fight. So he is christened with his fighting name, branded, and set free to roam the plains for another two years or more.

In the midst of this rolling flat, Bacchus has a home, the renowned city of Jerez,—badly pronounced by Shakespeare, "Sherris," thus giving to the English-speaking world the word "sherry." Here is the nursery of this famous wine where, in overground cellars, *bodegas,* it is watchfully nourished from tender infancy to ripe old age. A hundred years produces a wine aptly christened "Methusaleh." Some still older is dedicated to the Twelve Apostles, who had pronounced as good "a little for thy stomach's sake and thine often infirmities." Many great emblazoned butts of various ages are reserved for those members of the royal family who practice the Apostolic precept. These regal casks are dedicated on the day of the birth of the royal infant, though Spanish politeness omits the birth dates on those barrels destined for the Infantas.

Jerez is a city of wine cellar after wine cellar, where thousands and hundreds of thousands of casks are ageing under vigilant guardian eyes. The very air is saturated with its rich aroma, and it is one of the cleanest, most prosperous little cities in all Spain, every building looking as though it had just passed from the hands of the *albañil* (whitewasher), dazzling the stranger with an overpowering air of well-being.

Of course we pay a visit to one far-famed *bodega,* where they do the honors with courtly courtesy—perilous honors, unless you take good heed of the morrow; for in your journeying, you will have been tendered thirty, perhaps forty glasses of every shade of golden brown, in whose amber laugh lurks magic powerful enough to bring back life to a dead man—or lose it to the living.

It was the wine-bibbing in late Visigoth days, so says history, with its sisters, Luxury and Licentiousness, that cankered the heart of a great nation. Certain it is that had the Visigoths retained their old-time warlike simplicity, Spain never would have had a Moorish invasion, but Destiny elected these degenerate days, here on the banks of the Guadalete which sweeps about Jerez, for fighting out the fate of Spain. A great assemblage, says the old chronicles, gathered on the plains. "Berbers armed with lance and spear, roving Bedouins on their fleetest steeds, their glossy coats hung with beads and charms; Ethiopians black as night; Nubians with matted hair, and men from Barbary and Tunis.

Tharyk was their leader. On landing he burned all the ships in which they had crossed the sea. "Behold," said he, pointing to the flames which ran swiftly along the wood of the light triremes, "there is no escape for cowards; we conquer or we die. Your home is before you!" And in the varying fortunes of the following day he would fling himself in front of any retreating troops, shouting, "Whither would ye fly? Forget not the impassable sea lies that way, while the sea of enemies in front can easily be passed. Follow me!" and he rode with them to victory, and to the lordship of Spain, which they retained many centuries.

Not a cloud, not even a trace of scudding fleece dims the dream blue of the sky. Beneath its perfect azure we first see Cádiz—an island of silver linked to earth by a thread of gold. The Greeks called this the city of Aphrodite, born of the foam of the sea, for out of the blue ocean rises Cádiz in a splendor of white stone and snowy marble, joined to the mainland by the slenderest strip of yellowed earth. It is the oldest colony in Spain, four hundred years old when Rome was founded; settled by Phœnician mariners eleven hundred years before the Christian era; the limit of the world for the ancients, the Tarshish of the Bible, where sailed the fleets of Solomon every three years. As we wind along the narrow causeway between the waves, where dance little fishing boats, with many great vessels swaying at anchor, and having a mind filled with such Old World recollections, it is hardly surprising that our eyes see only Roman triremes and a "silver fleet" that has just brought tribute from the New World.

But once past the fortified gateway, we are in a city of smiling newness that looks as if just come to life. Everything is well ordered and excessively neat, with an atmosphere of prim respectability quite at variance with the usual painted picture of that voluptuous city, which, when known as Gades, catered with lascivious dances to the blasé Roman voluptuaries, leaving to its women the present-day reputation of having *"las mas salerosos cuerpos de España"* (the most enticing bodies in Spain). Naturally we have no facts to prove this statement.

Imagine this picture without a cloud, the blue of heaven mingling with the blue of sea, and, floating in space, a "city of snow," where even the roofs are white, as are the *miradores* (view towers) rising high above, giving the impression of a city built upon a city. These *miradores,* originally built as lookouts from which the seafaring people might discern the approach of returning treasure-laden galleons, are in reality roof patios, where in the cool of the evening all the household gathers to breathe in the sea odors wafted from the enveloping ocean. For wherever you may be within the city, you are never far from the waters that surround her and that are vigilantly kept in place by rugged old ramparts built of uncut stone. Along these are strung the sheltered Alamedas and palm-grove parks, where the sea winds are shorn of all power for mischief.

Always the sea. She greets you in the market

place with her treasures exposed for sale in a shifting riot of color, the glow of which seems to light up the dark faces of the women who sell. There are violet cuttlefish, gilt-headed besugos with popping golden eyes, blue-striped sardines, brilliant red mullets, pink shrimps, green lobsters, and silver turbot. And behind stand the barelegged *muchachas* in short red petticoats, shouting their wares in a bedlam of noise.

Always the sea. The Capuchin convent overlooks it, guarding the Virgin of Cádiz—a vivid-looking shepherdess with flapping broadbrimmed straw hat, who beckons to her flock clambering up the flower-strewn hill, where for a moment she halts, bringing to this people closely hemmed in by water, a vision of woodland, wide plains, and pasture fields—the world "ever craving something not possessed."

Always the sea. We go to it after the world has wrapped itself in midnight mantle, when perhaps the water is sobbing among the rocks and the darkness brings the sky nearer, and the stars approach to whisper their eternal message. We stand alongside it at daybreak, watching the reds dissolve into yellow, tinging the higher buildings, while leaving the lower still in shade;

when the sun would leap up in the East, a gorgeous disk of gold, working its ever-changing miracle of color that drifts from gold to pink, the pink at last stealing away into nothingness. Over the sea, plane great white birds—Maeterlinck calls them "thoughts flying across the sea of memory." We follow them in their flight, until the gentle, peaceful lap of the waves lulls memory to sleep.

April 21

Soon after leaving the fortified gateway of Cádiz, we plunge into a swampy marsh where the still waters, caressed by the ever faithful sun of Andalusia, gleam like fragments of a broken mirror. In this desolate Isla de León the fugitive government of Spain during the War of Independence made its last stand under the protecting guns of the English fleet—the only place in all the Peninsula where safety could be guaranteed. Here was conceived in the minds of a few enthusiasts that constitution of freedom of which the great fault lay in being too far in advance of the country and the times. On the restoration of the monarchy it was quickly bottled up by Ferdinand with the jocose remark that "Spain is nothing but a flask of beer for which I must act as cork; without·me, all would go up in froth."

At our approach flocks of startled ducks rise with shrill cries from out the stagnant ponds, planing heavenward. The ocean has been enticed into these shallows, where the water evaporated by the sun leaves behind deep beds of salt. These, collected into huge pyramids of dazzling white, cover the lowland with what look like tents of a military encampment. Andalusians, who interpret all life in the language of religion, have named them the "Flower of Jesus."

We are never far from a glimpse of the sea and always in sight of history, which has woven this short stretch of coast into countless dramas staged from the legendary days of Hercules all the way down through the centuries to the battle of Trafalgar.

Trafalgar! What a dramatic picture that must have been—a long line of ships, every one riddled and torn with shells, covered with dead and dying, among whom lay the heroic Nelson, himself mortally wounded. Drifting alongside his helpless flagship was the dismantled vessel of the Spanish admiral, also at death's door, making ready, as he himself expressed it, to join

CADIZ

GIBRALTAR.

the greatest man the world had ever known. A splendid victory—and a "magnificent defeat."

And now Tarifa, where Europe and Africa draw most closely together, Europe's jutting point perfectly fitting into the break on the opposite shore, from which, eons ago, it was torn asunder. Barbary pirates used to keep watch from those sentinel towers of Tarifa still standing, and every passing sail was obliged to pay tribute. A most fitting source from which to derive the name of our modern robber—Tariff.

Washed by the sea, the old castle of Guzmán, el Bueno, has also withstood the ravaging hand of Time; even the moated wall of which the ancient poets sang is still intact. According to these quaint ballads, the nine-year-old son of Guzmán was brought before the castle by the besieging Moors, with the threat to kill him did his father not surrender the city. To this, the father answered by throwing his dagger at the feet of the Arabs, saying, after the fashion of the old-time hidalgoes of Spain:

Matádle con esta	Kill him with that,
Que mas quiero honor sin hijo,	I prefer honor without son
Que hijo con mi honor manchado.	To son with honor stained.

199

And a similar grim atmosphere pervades the entire city. There is something almost repellant in the tightly shut and closely latticed windows, the better so to protect beauty, whose dark eyes might flash too meaning glances at some wandering Frankish stranger. Indeed, there is scarcely a woman to be seen anywhere. The few that are on the streets are shrouded as are their African sisters, their heads covered so that only one eye can look out—and that one eye glares malevolently. In Tarifa, Time has unwound the wrappings of many centuries and stands before us in the garments of long ago.

We are on our way again, this time over hills that rise almost from the water's edge. Their slopes are covered with thousands of gnarled and twisted cork trees, that have been flayed of their thick spongy bark, leaving the stark, naked trees bleeding their lifeblood in clogs of crimson sap.

Mules in charge of some gayly clad muleteer and loaded with the produce of the woodland are slowly filing through the forest track to the music of their own tinkling bells. Long lines of oxen-drawn carts piled high with sheets of cork are creaking their way toward Algeciras, the drivers seemingly cheered by the noise of the greaseless wheels. But even though our road carries us into the depths of these wild, romantic hills, now peering into a deep gorge, now shooting up some dizzy height, we are ever sniffing the sea. Reaching the extreme summit, there unrolls before us the Straits of Gibraltar, the water sheet on which have been written some of the greatest stories in the history of man.

We can easily distinguish the faint purple outline of the Atlas Mountains, that mark the mysterious coast of Africa now wrapped in gossamer blankets of sea fog. When ripped apart, revealed to us will stand Abyle of the ancients, directly opposite the Punta de Europa (the Spur of Europe), the two points upon which Hercules set up his legendary pillars, after rending asunder the mountains which joined Africa to Europe. Here was the ancient limit of the world, the *ne plus ultra*.

Below us is Algeciras, whose life, though long—for Chaucer wrote of "the true knight who fought at Algecir"—lays claim to but one brief hour of real notoriety, and that during the Moroccan Conference of 1906, when the ex-Emperor of Germany rattled his sword in vain hysterical protest.

Three colors immediately impress the eye, the intense blue of the sky, the white-plastered house walls, and the green of the trees, through whose latticework of boughs the sun is pouring. And then just across the bay from this scented garden, the grim, gray tomb of the god of war, where, outstretched at full length, lies a mighty giant, sword in hand, in all the majesty of martial power. Bristling with artillery and dotted with the portholes of hidden batteries, the Rock of Gibraltar rises brutally, truculently, from out the quiet.

Here is England entirely at home: her red-coated soldiers with little caps perched over one ear, swagger stick in hand; her Bobbies, shining with soap and intense respectability; her women, manly in sport clothes; her London coaster wagons; her two-wheeled carts; her churches and her ale houses, with doors wide open, showing pictures of prize fights and horse races.

Great Britain's strong individuality has been indelibly stamped upon a foreign soil and upon a heterogeneous population. Conversant with all the languages of the Tower of Babel, the people speak only English when spoken to, whether they be the silent, sharp-eyed Jews, wearing dark-colored gabardines, the tall green-turbaned Moors in yellow slippers, the red-fezzed Moroccans, the Persian Orientals in European clothes, the smooth-tongued Greek, the birettaed Catalan, or Mr. Aboab from India.

And lest you forget that this is England's home, every evening at sundown a signal gun is fired, in warning that all who are not British subjects or supplied with special permission sealed with British approval must leave Gibraltar before the sun goes down. Then through the sentried gates, like operatives from some gigantic factory, pour the laborers of the day, lured from Spain by generous wage.

The second gun must find no stranger within the city walls. Indeed, it is a crime, punishable by heavy fine, for an alien to be born in exclusive English Gibraltar—this by way of trying to prevent prospective Spanish mothers from crossing the frontier and so claiming military exemption for their son-children. But old Mother Nature knows no law that forces her to distinguish between day and night, and a good American clerical friend tells us that on an afternoon's visit to Gibraltar, he was unexpectedly presented with twins, to the dismay of the household in which he was stopping. Only because of his

203

cloth was he let off with a light fine—the twins being counted as one. Every profession has its compensations.

Gibraltar owes its name to the one-eyed Berber who victoriously overran Spain in the early seven hundreds—Gebel Târik. Long neglected by Spain, as of no special importance, and feebly garrisoned, she fell an easy prey to one of England's marauding expeditions, and this gate of the Mediterranean became an English possession—"A post of power invaluable to friends and dreadful to enemies." What a thorn in the flesh of sensitive Spain, forever pricking her national pride!

Despite repeated military attacks and wordy battles of politicians, Gibraltar remains English, and probably will so remain—a little corner of Spain transformed into a little England. Here she will continue to live amid transplanted home customs and regular habits, for "Latitudes may change, but England never changes."

Governor's Lane and the office of the military secretary receives us most graciously, thanks to the kindly American consul. During our stay this gracious gentleman celebrates a notably unusual occasion for a United States representative

—the ninetieth family anniversary in this one diplomatic post, the present occupant succeeding his father and grandfather.

We are put in charge of a sergeant, stiff with all the starched importance of the non-commissioned officer. He soon unbends, however, under the warmth of the African sun, as we toil up the steep incline, where typically English, cold, gray stone houses clamber with us—so long as a house can find footing.

The defenses are wonderfully contrived. At every strategic nook and corner of this rugged precipice, behind concealing shrubbery, crouch watchful "bulldogs"—powerful cannon with a long-distance bite. Gibraltar babies, our sergeant lovingly calls them, and in the galleries tunneled through the living stone, reaching all vulnerable spots, are huge porthole openings overlooking the cliff, where other dogs of war show their teeth. Once astride the saddle of the "Rock," peering down its nearly perpendicular slopes, it looks just what it is, an almost impregnable stronghold.

And yet, so our sergeant tells us, not so many years ago it was nearly captured by a scouting troop of Spaniards, who managed in the darkness of the night to dig their way almost within reach of the summit garrison. Just in time the shrill cries of the Tarshish apes, frightened by the moving figures, gave warning. Phlegmatic England was roused to the sentimental pitch of voting to the apes, in appreciation, a monthly ration of thirty shillings worth of animal dainties. Was it not King Solomon, incidentally, who "had at sea a navy of Tarshish (Spain) which once in three years brought him gold, silver, and apes"?

From this airy height our eyes sweep over two seas—the Mediterranean and the Atlantic; over Africa—Morocco and Algiers; over Europe—as far as the mountain ranges of Ronda and the snow heights of the Sierras. Even as we gaze around, the glorious sun "plays alchemist," bringing beauty and light to all the dark places.

All but one—and there the shadows take on an ugly look, as along the line marking the end of England's possessions, fair-haired men pace back and forth with guns on their shoulders. Opposite, separated by only a narrow strip of deserted sand,—no man's land,—is another line of sentinels, Spain's black-eyed, sinewy soldiers. They too carry guns. Two nations face to face in perpetual malignant vigil.

April 22

On leaving little England, Spain's custom officers look us over—rather perfunctorily and very apologetically, as though between gentlemen such questions should never arise. The workmen returning from Gibraltar, however, are thoroughly handled from head to foot in rigid examination, for to smuggle from dutiless England into high-duty Spain is too beguiling a temptation ever to be resisted by such lovers of exciting adventure as are the Spaniards. Women show the greatest ingenuity in this battle of wits. There are no female inspectors, and consequently women are immune from too intimate a search. We notice one, apparently soon to become a mother, who in a loud voice is railing against inhuman England for forcing her to leave in such a condition. Her son, she shouts, will be born with a song of hate on his baby lips. A scorching invective to which the inspectors listen with approving nods. But once beyond the custom line and well out of sight of its officials, she takes from under her skirt two huge packages of tobacco, winking at us the while with a jubilant expression of victory. The church does not consider smuggling a sin against religion or morals, so long as it is done without bribery—at least, so we are told.

Just beyond is San Roque, the summer home of Gibraltar, perched on top of a mountain ridge, a perpetual nest of smugglers who apparently have no other occupation than to do nothing all day long. This they conscientiously pursue, sitting on a chair in front of some café, listlessly smoking and watching the clouds roll by.

All the way to Málaga our road skirts the sea, oftentimes so near that under a gale the devouring waters tumble over it, greedily swallowing a great hunk of earth to be carried back into its hungry maw. Every river of Spain apparently has chosen this beach as its playground—ten, twenty, thirty of them, within a few miles, are racing one another down to the Mediterranean in a mad dance that hollows out more big gaps. Some day these may be bridged, for the foundations are laid,—perhaps an arch or two—just enough to inspire hope for future generations. At the broad river Guadiaro, an enterprising peasant—three years passed in America may account for his spirit—has provided oxen to drag vehicles over the otherwise impassable ford. He also has a helper or two to carry foot passengers across on their shoulders. Nothing in this world is pleasant that is not spiced with variety.

To be all day in touch with the Mediterranean, when the sky has become that peaceful "pious blue like some nun's eyes," and the endless variety of color and action along the shore holds one fascinated, is a priceless experience. Along the hillsides, in violent contrast, yellow gorse flames through wide patches of poppies, waving the national colors of Spain. One dainty little village after another stretches out by the water's edge, like fair bathers resting in the sun. On the beach, their vivid skirts whipping in the breeze, fisherwomen stand with unconscious grace against some sea-battered old boat draped with rust-colored nets.

All too soon Málaga extends the hand of welcome. Yes, all too soon, for while the sea always brings beauty to a city, it also leaves an unpleasant scum behind. True of all seaports the world over, Málaga, the oldest, most famous port on the Mediterranean, proves no exception. We are continually pestered by shifty-eyed individuals inviting us to a rendezvous with a frail beauty of Málaga, the daughter or wife of some well-known personage, they whisper, who is supposed to be passing the afternoon with a friend. This is said to be a common enough practice in Spain to call for passing notice, and giving point to the Spanish proverb that woman is better off at home with a broken leg. In this commercial city the men absent themselves all day, and the women, after early mass, are supposed to spend the rest of their time on flower-decked balconies talking to canaries, leading an orientally guarded life that sometimes forces them to copy their ingenious Eastern sisters in attracting admirers. And there is a very considerable sediment of orientalism remaining in this detached fragment of Africa, with its habitual indolence, its religious fanaticism, its indifference to pain in themselves or others. It shows itself also in the rich ivory complexions and in those soft *malaguenas,* which we Anglo-Saxons are wont to term Spanish music, though in reality they are Arabian melody. All the characteristic seductive, exotic charm of the province is in harmony with the city of everlasting summer and of almost everlasting sun.

In so commercial a center one would expect modern commercial methods, but when, in need of money, we visit Málaga's largest bank, it is to find the same patience-trying system as is in vogue elsewhere in Spain.

A somnolent clerk takes our letter of credit and disappears, apparently to finish his interrupted nap, for it is fully fifteen minutes before he reappears, and then only to carry the troublesome document to another clerk, who scrutinizes it and us with unconcealed suspicion. From him it passes to a seemingly higher authority, who merely glances at it with an expression of jaded aversion, lighting a fresh cigarette which he smokes to the finish, before deigning to read it over. But the end is not yet. Still another wearied official must give his stamp of approval, and there is another long "confab" before we receive a brass disk punched with a number which we are told will be called as soon as the cashier is able to count out the required money. At the end of a further quarter of an hour, when we are about beginning to doubt the cashier's ability, we hear a tired voice chanting the long-awaited numerals—and forty minutes have run away, down the river of Time.

April 23

We are passing through a paradise of sunshine and flowers, where the fig trees are already beginning to fruit, the almonds are ablossom, and the pomegranates are making ready their

211

royal rubies. And the vines of Xarab are about
to put forth their leaves in promise of more
wine—a wine so delicious that the Arabs, to
whom wine is forbidden by the Koran, would
pray to Allah, begging that before they died
they might be granted just one drink of
Málaga's nectar.

And then, suddenly, from out this flowering
plain over which the sun is breaking in billows
of fire, the mountains come to meet us, gloomily
barren and thickly strewn with huge bowlders,
called by the peasants the "tears of Christ." The
road is lonely, singularly deserted, not a thing
to testify to man's existence save straying cattle
noisily shaking their silvery bells. Just the setting for the adventurous tales of smuggling
Andalusia, or for the theatrical scenes for some
handsome villain—and Mérimée made these
mountains the hunting ground of "Don José,"
who lost his soul to "Carmen."

In the midst of this amphitheater of mountains lies a cultivated plain out of which springs
an isolated spur, that some knight-errant giant,
like Don Quixote, mistaking it for an enemy,
has blindly attacked. With his mighty sword
he has hacked it in two, splitting it from top to
bottom. Two Rondas perch on these eagle

heights—the old and the new—joined by an aërial bridge, from whose parapets, guarded by iron grills, we look down over the sheer precipice upon a sight, of its kind, unequaled in the world. A wild cascade sprays the rock-choked bed of a river hundreds of feet below, writhing and foaming through this mighty gorge, dug ever deeper and deeper with the passing of time. Boiling and bubbling, it leaps toward the far-away Moorish mills, whose wheels it turns as of old; then more quietly it drops into the farther plain, meandering through toy farms where Lilliputian figures toil—but always laughing gayly, loudly. A kindly-faced old woman points out the goat path that straggles down to the river bed, and in acceptance of our proffered coin, she thanks us with that beautiful Spanish phrase of leave-taking, *Vaya usted con Dios* (Go with God). I can assure you that several times when scrambling over the immense rocks below, slippery with the tumbling water, I thought I should.

We manage to clamber almost to the foot of the Casa del Moro, within which is concealed a rude underground stairway leading to the town above,—so as to obviate all danger of water famine in time of war. During the siege of Ferdinand the Catholic, Christian captives toiled up and down these steps day and night, carrying water to their Moorish masters, whose fierce king drank only from the skulls of enemies; cutting off their heads and making them into goblets inlaid with splendid jewels.

Along the edge of the cliff, clinging to its precipitous sides, can be seen the plain white walls of oriental-looking houses, with windows grated by fanciful *rejas,* the doors of massive oak, iron bound and studded with knobs of brass. In the hands of the occupants as they leave the house are clutched big keys, too big for pocket, picturing for us the story of the Moors, who, when forced to leave, are said to have carried away their door keys against the time they should reclaim this long-time stronghold. But they will never come back.

9

Toledo, the Spanish Rome

We are back in Seville. With the dawn of day we cross the fabled waters of the Guadalquivir into the gypsy quarter of Triana, where every cross street is one of nocturnal adventure, the home of those sulky, animalistic creatures with the smoldering instinct of tiger cats. At this hour the streets are deserted, voices are quiet, the throb of the guitar and the maddening click of the castanets are silenced. Triana sleeps. There is nothing to disturb or distract the mind from harking back to the days when Seville was known as Sephela, and the Phœnicians were wont to carry through these very streets their dusky goddess, Astarte, the idol of love and fruitfulness. Black-haired and blackbodied, her bosom covered with ropes of amulets and shells, she was borne through Triana on a platform, followed by an adoring multitude, just as are the images of the Virgin today. It was the custom then, as now, for the people to prostrate themselves on the approach of the deity. That day all did so but two—two Christian damsels, Rufina and Justa, sellers of earthen jars. They refused to bow their heads, and were stoned to death by the infuriated multitude; later to be rewarded by being beatified into patron saints of Seville, in whose cathedral hang their portraits, painted by Goya. Not very saintly looking, it must be confessed, lending credibility to the story that Goya employed two of Triana's beautiful "fallen angels" as his models.

A glorious birth is sunrise! The sky becomes a symphony of color, passing from brightest red to golden orange, drifting from gold to pink, the pink becoming a blush green, gradually subsiding into lilac, coloring for a moment the great spaces lying along the horizon; almost beautifying the near-by village of Itálica that spreads out its rags and its ruins with a haughty pride worthy of the birthplace of three of Rome's great emperors.

But even under the rays of a joyful sun there is a tangible sadness in a land naked of trees; a brooding melancholy that so depresses our cheerful fellow traveler that when we stop for a moment at Castillejo and are told that Hernando Cortéz, the conqueror of Mexico and the discoverer of California, died there, he exclaimed, "My God, I don't wonder!"

It is much the same here as in the adjoining plain of "La Mancha," which well merits the Arabian name of Dry Desert—monotonous and solitary, with nothing to soften or break the blinding light. It is even lonelier now than in Cervantes' time, for then there were bands of wandering monks, courtly robbers, errant damosels, and sighing princesses. Of all this phantom company, the giant windmills at which Don Quixote spurred with lance at rest alone remain, their white wings still turning and turning without cessation, in insolent defiance, according to every fantasy of the wind. Now and then there are a few patched and tattered figures following teams of oxen in the constant war between man and this dry, parched earth, a soil that shows dark red as though fevered by the burning sun. All the plowed land of Spain seems red of one shade or another, but here it is the red of blood, boiling with the ardor of heaven on fire.

But once over the mountain barrier and well into the harsh, savage province of Estremadura, there is a complete change like the quick shifting of the scenes of a theater. The sky becomes as ungracious as the landscape, and the people sullen, where before all were smiling. The welcome that awaits us at the low-raftered, stuffy inn of Mérida, the celebrated capital of Lusitania, is one of cold indifference, a moldering chill, and an overpowering odor of the past—a past largely of strong oil and stronger garlic. However, all of Mérida lives among strong odors of antiquity bequeathed to her by Rome—Roman aqueducts, Roman bridges, Roman forums, Roman coliseums—crumbling masses of reddish brown, colored by the rain and winds of time. The only "remains" that show no hint of decay are the oven of Santa Eulalia, which is piously believed to be where that infant martyr was roasted to death in A.D. 303, the legend prettily describing how, at the moment of death, her soul in the form of a white dove issued from her mouth and flew to heaven.

Early this night we hear a noisy shuffling back and forth in front of the inn, the street each moment becoming more and more congested with a laughing throng, all carrying some sort of kitchen utensil and a long-handled ladle or spoon. Our curiosity aroused, we follow the people into the well-filled plaza, where someone harangues the crowd that forms into line, marching to the outskirts of the city. There they quietly surround an old gabled cottage whose lights are already extinguished. At a sign there commences a serenade—a frightful, hideous din from hundreds of dish pans, sauce-pans, milk pans. bread pans, furiously beaten to the accompaniment of deriding groans and shrill catcalls. This is the village protest against the marriage celebrated that afternoon, of a seventy-year-old Don Juan to a sixteen-year-old girl, to be repeated every night, lasting all night, until the old man wearies of a purchase he will not be allowed to enjoy.

Much of the way to Toledo is through a boundless prairie, almost trackless except for the one silver thread winding over the undulating country in long, straight stretches that reveal from afar the occasional traveler astride his dusky-coated donkey. In the days of Pizarro, the conquistador of Peru, who was born here in Trujillo, this country was rich with loot from the Incas, but the lure of gold took thousands to America. The deserted land became the home of wandering flocks of sheep, in charge then, as today, of fierce, wild-looking creatures, more beast than man, their bodies covered with rough, undressed sheepskin, their scowling faces almost concealed by long, matted hair. For months at a time these shepherds wander over the lonely heaths, their only companions enormous wolf-hounds and their beloved *navaja,* a dirklike knife, with which they chip bread or kill a man with equal felicity.

Lovers of melancholy could here enjoy to their heart's content the pleasure of being sad. It is an ideal place to hide from the world, as Charles the Fifth decided when he chose the picturesque Yuste Cloisters of this dreary Estremadura in which to fret away his declining years. Don Pedro the Cruel chose the castle of Talavera de la Reina, through which we are passing, as the most isolated place he could find for Blanche of Bourbon, his wife of a day, to spend her honeymoon, in solitary exile, being diabolically accused of having accorded favors to the knightly Don Fadique, who had acted for Pedro as his proxy in marriage.

But waiting for us at the bottom of the valley are the historical walls of the roofless palace of Benavente, a smoke-blackened monument of Castilian loyalty.

"No one shall enter the doors of my palace who is not cleaner than the sun, nor shall it be profaned by a traitor to his country and his king, even though he be a cousin to a king." So declared El Conde de Benavente as he denied hospitality to the powerful Duke of Bourbon. The Duke, outraged, went in anger to Emperor Charles, who was then in Toledo, accused Benavente, and demanded reparation. Charles owed much to the Duke, so he promised satisfaction and ordered Benavente to appear before him.

The venerable Prince hastened to salute his monarch, falling to his knee in profound deference. After requesting him to rise, the Emperor intimated that it was his wish that El Conde should lodge the Duke of Bourbon in his palace of Toledo.

It was with deep respect that Benavente replied: "Sire, I am your vassal, and what you order, I fulfill with my life, but do not touch my honor. If it is your will that he of Bourbon should occupy my house and profane my walls, it shall be, but when he leaves and before I re-enter, I must purify it with fire." With this he kissed the royal hand and took his leave.

A few days later the Duke took up his residence in the palace of Benavente. But the night he departed, the valley of the Tagus was alight

with a fierce fire that devoured the palace towers
and consumed in flames the riches of the house
of Benavente.

April 28

And when Nebuchadnezzar, the king of Baby-
lon, destroyed Jerusalem, the Jews, the Bible
tells us, fled to Tarshish (the scriptural name of
Southern Spain), calling the city of their refuge
"Toledoth."

Well-authenticated history proves that the
Jews were in Toledo before the Spaniards,
before the Moors, before the Visigoths, and
before the Romans. The old city is wrapped in
garments of mystic Hebrew legend, with more
of romantic lore to its credit than any other city
of Spain. Indeed, it names Adam as its founder,
though the more modest savants claim Noah,
who, after his Ararat experience, would
certainly choose a rocky height such as this for
his place of abode. Another charm the city
holds is that the great granite hill upon which
Toledo rests has been carved by the mighty river
Tagus into the form of a giant horseshoe, that
attractive emblem of good fortune to all wan-
derers in any country the world over. The
waters have bitten deep into the living stone,

leaving a perpendicular mass of rock on all sides but one—a brutal cut (Tajo) that gives its name to the stream.

It was, however, this very river Tagus that brought ill fortune to the Goths. The first springs of great events, like those of great rivers, are often mean and little, as Swift says, and it is an historic fact that the chance sight of the fair maiden Florinda bathing in the river Tagus, just below Saint Martin's bridge, brought the Arab invasion that sounded the death knell of the Visigoths. The story is much like that of King David, who, in the cool of the evening, walked on the roof of his palace, and saw the woman Bathsheba bathing herself. The woman was very beautiful to look upon, and although she was the wife of Uriah the Hittite, David took her unto himself. But the thing David had done displeased the Lord and he brought trouble upon David.

When Don Roderick, the last of the Visigoth kings, reigned in Spain, there was not a Moor in all the country. At that time Don Julian, the father of Florinda, himself half royal, was in command of the army which held the enemy in Africa at bay. Without the presence and support of Don Julian, the Moors would pour like

223

a torrent into the land, rich with rivers and pastures, which for so many years they had longed to possess. But Don Julian never once swerved in his loyalty to Roderick, proving his great esteem for the King by confiding to his protection, as was the custom in those days, his daughter Florinda, beautiful beyond words. She was to be a handmaiden of the court while he was absent at his post in Ceuta, the strategic city on the African shore.

Not long after Don Julian's departure it happened that one early eventide, after a day of fiery heat, Florinda with a band of fair damsels, all maidens of the court, went to the leafy garden of sweet perfume in search of a cooling breeze. This garden, overhanging the river, descended in low-terraced steps to the very brink of the water. No sooner were the maidens within the seclusion and shelter of the palm fronds than they all threw aside their light draperies and bathed in the refreshing waters of the dark Tagus. When tired of this sport, they stretched themselves upon the moss-covered banks, comparing with girlish vanity their delicately limbed bodies, to see which was the most beautiful. The auburn-haired Florinda surpassed the others, being, as the old chanson, whimsically relates, "most bewitching altogether."

While thus innocently playing, Fate takes Don Roderick out of the Alcázar Palace to enjoy the evening freshness. He hears the sound of happy laughter and walks down to the tower, now a mass of ruins, and from one of the latticed windows he sees the undraped figure of Florinda.

The consequences are historic. Insane from passion and forgetful of all knightly honor, he allows brute violence to conquer when persuasion was of no avail.

In despair, the dishonored girl wrote the miserable news to her father, who at that moment was leading the Visigoth army against the Moorish hosts in far-away Ceuta. She implored vengeance upon her betrayer, saying, "Alas, my father, your lamb has been trusted to a wolf."

On reading the fatal tidings Don Julian swore a terrible revenge, not only against the King, but against Spain, the scene of his dishonor. He went to Mousa, the Sultan of the Arabs, and offered to betray his country and his King. When the Sultan learned of the King's infamy, he blamed not Don Julian, but put him in high command, and sent a great army across the

straits to Spain. Near Jerez was fought the
battle of Guadalete that decided the fate of the
Peninsula for centuries to come.

Many of the invading army were by faith
Jews, whose progenitors, years before the time
of Solomon, had swept over western Africa,
intermarrying with the Berber tribes. To this
day Berber names show an obviously Hebrew
origin; for example, Yocoub for Jacob, Ibra-
him for Abraham, and Haroun for Aaron. It
was quite natural, therefore, when the victorious
Berbers appeared before the gates of Toledo
that the inhabitants of similar faith should welcome them joyfully, and be treated by the conquerors, not as conquered, but as friends. For
many, many years the Jews played a conspicuous
part in the life of Toledo, enjoying an immunity
such as they found nowhere else. Indeed, they
were free, even after the Spaniards had driven
out the Moors, to build temples, where they
might pray to God in their own way—a forbear-
ance due to the primitive Christian belief that
they were of the tribe of Israel whose High
Priest had sent a letter to Jerusalem protesting
against the crucifixion of Christ, and who, when
asked if Jesus should live or die, alone
responded, "Let him live."

It was after nearly four centuries of Moorish rule that Toledo fell into the hands of the Spaniards, opening her gates in the year 1085 to the victorious army of Alfonso of Castile. The first Christian banner to pass the entrance portal was that of the Cid, ever in the forefront in all Spanish victories.

Seated on his white charger, Babieca, he rode proudly down the Calle del Arrabel, going by the Puerta del Sol, that magnificent Arab arch reflecting in its rose-tinted stone the blaze of the sun, and then over the hill, up the narrow, twisting roadway that led to the little mosque which had begun its life as a Gothic church. But hardly had he passed the entry door, when his horse Babicca stopped short, snapping his bridle and falling to his knees on the rough cobbles. Though always before obedient to the voice of his master, he refused to move until the Cid, at last realizing that he was dealing with the supernatural, ordered his followers to investigate. Not until they began to dig into the façade of the church close to where he knelt, would Babieca rise to his feet. There, deeply imbedded within the wall, they unearthed a crucifix, before which a light was burning brightly—a cross and lighted lamp that had been hurriedly secreted by the Goths three hundred and seventy years before, when the besieging Moors had forced them out of the city.

So they named this church "Christ of the Light," *El Cristo de la Luz,* and there Alfonso, and the Cid, together, heard their first mass in conquered Toledo. Mass over, King Alfonso presented to the church, in memory of this miraculous event, his battle shield, a black cross on crimson ground, and he ordered a white stone to be set into the pavement just where the horse Babieca fell on his knees. Both these reliques remain to this very day, to the discomfiture of unbelievers. And the little mosque, the oldest building in Toledo, despite time and the desecrating hand of man, is still a perfect gem of oriental workmanship, reminiscent of Cordova.

But to continue the story of the Jews, which makes one of the most interesting chapters in the book of Toledo. Right in the heart of Judería, just out of the plaza of that name, is the oldest Jewish synagogue, now known as Santa María la Blanca (the White Saint Mary), a name given it when the church was converted into a home for repentant Magdalens. In the days of its glory the synagogue was ceiled with the cedar of Lebanon, the floor covered with the sacred

228

soil of Palestine, and the walls enriched by the genius of the Moorish builders whose splendid art speaks with the same eloquence whether in mosque, synagogue, or cathedral. While Santa María Blanca has suffered sorely, nothing can rob beauty of its innate sweetness.

In this same ancient quarter is another synagogue, El Tránsito, located where the dwellings were of the meanest appearance, hiding their luxury behind sordid exteriors, feigning poverty so as to save their stores of wealth from taxation. This was built by the wealthy Samuel Levy, the Rothschild of those times, the friend and treasurer of Pedro the Cruel, until that bloody monarch relieved him at once of his money and his head. It was erected in the days of the Jew's greatest prosperity, and is superbly trellised with honeycombed carvings that in delicacy and richness are in no way inferior to the best in the Alhambra. Above the holy of holies, where the rabbis expounded the law, and shrouded by an Eastern veil of stucco, is a twining arabesque singing in Kufic letters a pæan of joy: "Now hath God delivered us from the power of our enemies and since the days of our captivity never had we a safer refuge. But nothing endures except mutability."

From the synagogue runs a quiet little street named in honor of the distinguished Hebrew, Calle de Samuel Levy, leading up to the palace built by him when in full enjoyment of power and influence. This man, mighty among his people, was one of the most prominent and picturesque in those troubled dramatic days, cleverly exploiting the needs and weaknesses of his master, Pedro, who continually needed money to carry on the incessant struggle against his illegitimate brothers. But the day came when, believing that gold was the axle on which turned the world, and therefore making him stronger than kings, he proved too heavy a taskmaster, drawing to himself the hatred of Pedro. Or perhaps it was only his enormous riches that excited the cupidity of the King. At all events, the once powerful Hebrew was arrested, and all his property confiscated. "And they found in the subterranean vaults of Levy's palace heaps and heaps of gold, taller than a man of average height."

Then the storm burst, and robbery was followed by a series of cruel persecutions. The end of the drama came when San Vincente Ferrar, "the servant of a Jew, the disciple of Him who was called Love," aroused the people of Toledo to such a pitch of fury that they began to massacre the Jews. In terror they appeared before their sovereign, offering thirty thousand ducats annually as the price of their protection. While the King was hesitating, the insatiable Torquemada entered the council room. He boldly upbraided the King, saying that Judas Iscariot sold his master for thirty pieces of silver, and you would sell him anew for thirty thousand. Though others spoke up, bidding the King take heed what he did to the Jews, "for whosoever touched them is like one who touches the apple of the eye of Jesus, for they are his flesh and blood," Torquemada prevailed. His influence was so great that later he persuaded the Catholic sovereigns to sign a decree of expulsion, and today if any of the proscribed race still live in Toledo, they cover their origin under the cloak of Castile.

And so, in consequence, the palace of Levy—where once was stored the fabled wealth of Solomon; through whose nail-studded door were passed thousands upon thousands of moneybags to help maintain Pedro, the friend of Israel, in power; in whose upper chambers were enacted the scenes so vividly painted by Balzac in his story of the master miser—is today known only as the house of El Greco, that most original of all painters, who lived and died there. It no longer has the appearance of a laboratory of golden alchemy, but that of an artist's home—a garden beautiful, within hearing of the voice of the Tagus, with ivy-covered walls, masses of blossom, a tiny courtyard with quaint walls, and a rambling wooden gallery that leads to a museum of painted treasure more precious than gold.

Within this palace was painted that marvelous canvas, "The Burial of Count Orgaz," that hangs in the church of Santo Tomé, a little way from the artist's home, up the steep side street. The painting is of a series of eager faces peering into the vague unknown, oblivious to everything except the barrenness of life. It is said to embody much of the Spanish soul, and all of El Greco's, who became more Spanish than the Spanish themselves, and should properly have been called El Toledano rather than El Greco. A mad painter he was, they tell you in Toledo, merely because he was a genius with a craving for originality. He displayed, perhaps it is true, something of morbidness in his unusual, livid blacks and ashen whites, but in his portraits he caught the peculiar dignity of the Spanish hidalgo, making them live and speak. Proud and conscious of his sometimes unappreciated talent, he was in frequent dispute with his Mæcenas patrons, and, like a true Don Quixote of painting, even engaged in legal battle with the powerful cathedral when they refused his beautiful altarpiece, "Casting Lots for Christ's Raiment."

Like so many of the churches in Spain, the cathedral is almost invisible amid the many houses that shoulder up against it as though anxious to keep it hidden from sight. But seeking to make amends, she opens wide a door of welcome at the foot of almost every one of the many narrow, twisting passages that lead to this "Mistress of Toledo," rising from the very heart of the city in unrivaled pomp and splendor.

When the Moors surrendered to Alfonso and the Cid, they stipulated that they should retain their mosque. This, Alfonso, tolerant by nature and too recently in power to be certain of its duration, gladly allowed. But during his first absence from the city, the Queen, left in full control, was taken with strange scruples and sent for the archbishop, asking him if there were no means of seizing the mosque, formerly Christian, from the hands of the pagans, without breaking the King's word. The Jesuit, so says the chronicle, fell on his knees giving thanks to God for so inspiring the Queen, and he assured her that an earthly promise should never stand in the way of heavenly duty. That very day they went to the mosque, threw out into the street all the sacred objects of Islam, and set up an altar, a crucifix, and an image of the Virgin. King Alfonso, on hearing of the outrage upon his honor, hurried back to Toledo, vowing to punish those who had made him break his royal word. But the clever Arabs, with a perfect understanding of the human heart, knew that the King would ever look upon them as the cause of the sorrow that would follow stern retribution, "for he who kills today, repents tomorrow." They begged the King to pardon the evildoers, saying that they would voluntarily renounce the mosque, knowing that the other conditions of surrender would be held sacred. Thus they were able to live in peace with the King for many years, though the church remained Christian from that time forth.

The cathedral as we know it is of most imposing size, one of the finest and largest in the world. It required nearly three hundred years to build and was constructed at the time when

Spain reached the climax of her power and opulence. Armies of sculptors, painters, and workers in metal came from home and abroad, showering this great cathedral with the riches of their genius; writing for future generations immortal phrases expressed in gold, silver, and splendid marble. The first precious metal that Columbus sent from the New World was sent here, to be followed by countless treasures from popes, cardinals, princes, and all the great ones of the earth. Filling the cathedral is such a hoard of wealth that the words of Solomon could well be used, "riches and wealth such as none have had before thee, neither shall any after thee have the like." It is so incomparable an art museum that the jeweled contents dim the glories of the wondrous casket.

The cathedral was dedicated to the Virgin, who by way of gratitude came down from heaven to attend first mass, sitting in the cardinal throne of the beatified Ildefonso. It was he who had championed her immaculate honor before the early skeptics, and later she covered the saint's shoulders with a chasuble made of the cloth of heaven. Over the spot where she first alighted, near the open center of the church, is a Gothic chapel, railed in by a golden reja. This

235

protects the stone now deeply worn by the countless fingers thrust between the heavy bars reverently to touch the footsteps of the Virgin, in
search of the promised release from three hundred years of purgatory. Fingers bony and
and trembling with age, they are for the most
part, their owners, with the snow of time on their
heads, near the end of their earthly goal. But
there are other fingers, white and well rounded
in the mold of youth, seeking another sort of release. These girlish fingers drop within the
shrine a long or a short pin, according to their
desire for a tall or short husband; but long or
short, the pin is always accompanied by a piece
of money for a rich one.

Buried in the shadow of the farthest corner is
another notable shrine, possibly the only chapel
of its kind within Roman Catholic walls, for the
mass sung here daily is not the Gregorian mass
of Rome, but the Mozarabic ritual, the primitive
Apostolic mass of the early Goths. The Mo-
zarabe or Mixtarab was the name for Goths who
were willing to remain under Moslem rule so
long as they could retain their Christian worship. The religiously fanatical Spaniards on
capturing Toledo tried their best to suppress

this ritual, but the opposition was so great that according to the customs prevailing in those days, appeal was finally made to "the Judgment of God." Two bulls christened Rome and Muzarabe were opposed to each other in battle, and when the champion of Rome was defeated, two knights took up the gauntlet, one in dazzling white, mounted on a white charger, the other raven black from casque to toe, the defender of Gothic rites. At the first tilt Rome was unhorsed. But even then the Spaniards were not satisfied, and insisted upon a trial by fire. So a great pyre was built in the Plaza Zocodover, upon which were laid the two contending missals. When a torch set the fagots ablaze, the book of Rome was reduced to ashes, while the old Gothic parchment tome, bound in iron, with metal clasps, passed the ordeal successfully. And so it happens that one very early morning of this twentieth century, in a coldly pure Gothic chapel, we are privileged to listen to the original simple litany of the primitive Goths chanted by a sweet-voiced priest, while his acolyte with a long rod of silver turns the pages of the monumental book as it rests on the high altar. How long the Roman church will allow within its own walls this daily indifference to forms of adoration that mean so much to it, no man can tell.

Most of the art wonders of this sanctuary of the muses can unfortunately be seen only at a loss of the religious emotion which this beautiful church in moments of repose must always give. One must tramp side by side with a horde of blatant "trippers" from chapel to chapel, all of which are enclosed by heavy grilles of thick bars like cages of wild beasts, and to which admittance is charged. If one could only wander there in the quiet hours of the night, when from the myriad tombs of princes, kings, and cardinals who made history there arise spectral forms to take part in a ghostly mass of soundless liturgy! If the Zolaesque pen of Blasco Ibañez is to be believed, after nightfall a band of protecting wild dogs used to be let loose behind the closed doors of the cathedral—from which naturally follows the popular name of the day guardians at the present time, *Azotaperras* or "dog beaters."

Strange that for the English-speaking world Blasco Ibañez should be practically the only interpreter of Spain, who seems to consider him the very least of her great ones. As time goes on, he appears to be less and less in sympathy

with the Spanish ideals so firmly upheld by
Valle Inclan, that polished novelist ever true to
the Spanish tradition that good form requires an
intellectual to be somewhat poverty-stricken.
What a contrast is Ibañez who, only a day or two
since, rushing through Madrid, stated that he
found his now enormous earnings very natural,
and wished to increase them. "The two au-
thors," he went on to say, if quoted accurately
by the newspapers, "who earn the most money in
the world, are Rudyard Kipling and I—but no,
there is a third, Wells. We are the three who
gain the most. Now I have more than a million dollars. I receive a thousand for a short
story. The editors of the United States cable
me, asking for articles on all sorts of subjects.
My opinion is of great weight. Thus I live the
life of a prince and a slave. Prince with my
motor cars and my palace on the Riviera; slave
because I continue working, writing novels while
dictating short stories to my secretary.

"Perhaps because I love Spain so much I visit
her so little. A month there leaves me with
scratches and torn garments, for Spain to me is
full of nails, of pricks, and broken glass.

"No, Spanish politics do not interest me in
the least, I have more power in the world with

my novels than Spain itself. In Spain everything is a farce. I have open to me the newspapers of the world, and if ever anything is done to place Spain in harmony with the world, I shall not fail to take part. In the meanwhile I am going on with my new series of novels, not to vindicate Spain, for axioms do not require demonstrations, and that our country has played one of the principal rôles in the world's comedy, tragedy, and drama—until we disappeared through a trapdoor, losing our independence when we won the War of Independence—is long ago acknowledged. My work is in the United States of America where Captain Cook, who was made into sandwiches in the Sandwich Islands, is better known than Magellan, Cortes, Balboa, or any other of the hundred Iberians who demonstrated that the world is as round as an orange."

The rambling, twisting streets of Toledo, like some mysterious labyrinth, squeeze in between high cañons of somber, silent houses, from out whose enormous doors, studded with constellations of huge knobs of chiseled bronze, one expectantly awaits some intellectual-faced cardinal, hidalgo in velvet, or knight in chased armor.

So narrow are these tortuous lanes, absolutely impassable for carriages, that, leaning out of the window on one side, it is possible to shake hands easily with a person leaning from the other. And the projecting balconies, leaving visible but a tiny patch of sky, are so close together as easily to permit aërial familiarities were it not for the heavy bars, whose severity is softened by fragrant blossoms peeping from between the cold iron.

One crooked alley follows another, always, however, zigzagging its winding way in the direction of some open plaza, such as the ancient Arab market of Zocodover, the center of Toledan life. This plaza, planted with little trees, is surrounded by high houses whose sunbaked fronts contrast strongly with the whiteness of the awnings hanging low before the little windows in tent-like forms. It cannot be very different from what it was in the seventeenth century, for Cervantes gives a description fitting it so well that we are almost able to go to the very bookstall where he bought that parcel of papers containing the history of Don Quixote written by Cid Hamil, the Arabian. And going out through the Puerta, a little way down the calle leading to the river, is easily found the Inn of

Blood, *Posada de la Sangre,* where he lived and
wrote of the prettiest scullery wench ever
known, who "had the sun in one cheek and the
moon in the other; the one is made of roses and
the other of carnations, and between them both
are lilies and jasmine—a dainty morsel for some
archbishop."

Stopping for a moment, we look into the ancient courtyard, surrounded on all sides by a
time-stained, wooden sleeping gallery upheld
on stone pillars that have long served as hitching
posts for the weary mules. Even now they are
dejectedly resting against the supporting posts,
and, gathered together in one corner, we see a
number of grumbling muleteers watching while
mine host pours out a scanty measure of oats for
their hungry beasts. Then from out the smoke-
darkened archway steps a young girl who asks,
"What may it please you to want, Señor?" just
as Castanza in the story. When we tell her, she
gives an understanding smile and bids us enter.

Our way, however, is down to the Puente de
Alcántara, that superb bridge of entry into the
warlike city. It is crowded, as usual, with a
score of water carriers, who are trying as best
they can to relieve the drought in thirsty Toledo.
Laden on poor, half-starved brutes or packed

RONDA. THE OLD TOWN ON THE HEIGHTS, THE BRIDGE
SPANNING THE TAJO, AND OLD MILLS ON THE SIDE OF
THE GORGE.

THE OLD ROMAN BRIDGE AT TOLEDO, LEADING TO THE CITY. THE ALCÁZAR ABOVE.

into some creaking handbarrow, they bring in earthen jars a never ending stream from the spring across the river.

From here a road leads around to El Cristo de la Vega—a little chapel behind flower-covered walls, guarding the famous statue of Christ, nailed to the cross, with one hand wrenched free, holding it outstretched by his side. Many years ago a poor working girl of Toledo and her lover, strolling through these meadows in the cool of the evening, stopped at Cristo de la Vega (Christ of the Meadows) to pledge their troth. Standing before the Crucifix, her inamorato solemnly made his promise of marriage, permitting them to live together without further ceremony. But when in the course of time the girl found herself with child, the man, wearied, denied ever having made such a promise, and the poor girl in disgrace, fled back to the little chapel where their troth had been plighted, seeking comfort. There the priest to whom she confessed tried to counsel her, asking her if she had no possible proof, no witness to her betrothal. As she sorrowfully answered that she had none, the church was filled with a radiant light, the arm of Christ fell from the cross, and a voice was heard to say: "I testify."

Climbing back to the city and over the fortified bridge of Saint Martin, which is near the Bath of Florinda, the road winds to the heights beyond the Tagus. From here we look down upon the roof-covered hill, confined within brutal walls of rock, torn asunder by the foaming river. Towering far above the forest of spires and pinnacle, shooting skyward, are "the priest and warrior" of the city—the divine cathedral and the stern, forbidding Alcázar, that citadel which has withstood so many sieges; within whose walls the great ones of the world have lived and laughed; through whose massive, barred windows countless prisoners, pining for liberty, have wistfully looked out upon the same scenery spread out before us today.

From the cloudless, vaporless sky—a steel-blue, like the well-tempered Toledo blades—pours a scintillating fire upon the massed roof tops, coloring them with matchless tints and drawing from the profusion of wild flowers on the plain about us an aromatic perfume that embalms the air with a tantalizing fragrance. In no other part of the world, says the friend with us, is there such a confusion of sweet odors as escape from the "miracle flowers" of the Valley of the Virgin. He tells of one of the inhabitants of this valley who, long ago forced to flee from Spain because of some slight infraction of the law, crossed over to Africa, working as a slave among the Moors, by whom he was so much respected that he became the eyes of their blind Sheik. After testing his faithfulness, the all-powerful Mohammedan confided to his slave the secret that for long had buoyed him up with hope—the hope that one day he might be able to see, for a priest of the much-reviled Christians had once told him that if he could have sufficient faith, there grew in the Valley of the Virgin among the mountains of Toledo, a flower that would bring back his sight. He asked his slave to go there and pick one of every kind that grew. "If you bring back the healing one," he said, "I will give you anything you may ask, even to the half of my kingdom." The slave arrived in the Valley of the Virgin just at the time when the earth was singing with flowers. So many were there that it took full three days before he had plucked one of each kind. He returned to his master, and the old Sheik welcomed him with joy, plunging his trembling hands into the great sackful of flowers, pulling out, one by one, the half-dead blossoms which he eagerly passed before his sightless pupils.

245

When he had tried the very last one, and his eyes saw not, he wept bitterly, crying out that the Christian God did not believe his faith sufficient. Then the slave leaned down and untied his sandals, giving them to the Sheik, who rubbed their soles over his eyes. And the sandals having, unknown to their owner, trodden on the miracle flower, brought the light of heaven to the Sheik.

In this same valley there are said to be other miracle flowers, flowers that bring joy to the heart , peace to the soul, and love that passes all understanding.

10

Madrid—and the King!

April 30

A long, straight road, bumpy with ruts, like the abandoned furrows of some plow that has vainly sought fertile soil; a sullen, mournful desert, naked of trees, lashed by the sun. And then, suddenly, without warning, in the midst of waste desolation, an oasis, green with the greens of emeralds, lying in the fruitful embrace of the rivers Jarama and Tagus, whose marriage has clothed the sands with myriads of flowers, peopling it with giant trees, their interlacing branches bowing to the ground in luxuriant heaviness. This garden spot, Aranjuez, whose courtly charms are seen in many a Velásquez canvas, became the favorite retreat for royalty. It was at the height of its glory in the days of that picturesque scamp, the "Prince of Peace," Manuel Godoy, whose handsome figure and dashing manner gained not only the confidence of good-natured Charles the Fourth, but the love of his Queen, as well. When the too open scandal brought popular hatred, Godoy hid for hours from the fury of the mob, which finally found him, trembling with fear, rolled in a mat under the bed. They would have killed him then and there, had not the Queen, true to her lover, persuaded the deluded King to abdicate and turn over the reins of government to their son Ferdinand who headed the revolt, having long resented the favorite's insolence, his father's folly, and his mother's shame.

Nowadays Aranjuez is seldom used as a royal residence, and the palace is filled with silence and faded splendor; the gardens of roses and fantasy labyrinths of hedge are somewhat neglected. Silent also is the "marble cottage," known as the Casa del Labrador, as much a farmhouse as the Trianon of Versailles, after which it was modeled. With elaborate decorations and a medley of art beauties, it is quite worthy of another Pompadour. Silent also are the streets, deserted by their former splendor.

But one day, later, we see this sleepy little town awake and alive with animation, for that sport-loving king, Alfonso the Thirteenth, has transformed a part of this royal domain into a race course. Each spring he patrons two races, requesting the presence of all the social world, which brings the world at large in its train. Once again these splendid lawns are bright with gayly dressed courtiers, who, after a luncheon *al fresco* under the majestic elms, stroll over to the racing meet, and are scattered through the meadow land in seated groups. The royal hosts walk among the guests simply and unaffectedly, as at some garden party. They bow here and there to friends and acquaintances, stopping for a chat with some intimate, winning all hearts with their gracious words of welcome—kindly words that happily include ourselves.

That day the splendid highway to Madrid was lined with soldiers, permitting no stop except at a little isolated hill that unexpectedly springs from out the flat plain, a hill known as the Hill of Angels, whose summit is crowned with a colossal statue of Christ. This marks the geographical center of Spain and, with its inscription, beautifully testifies to the deeply religious heart of the country: "Jesus reigns in this land, and the King of Spain is his servitor."

May 1

In the broad Calle de Alcalá, Madrid's most frequented street, not a place of business is open —every window and door is barred; hotels, banks, and public buildings are surrounded by cordons of police; while just around the corners, somewhat hidden from sight, are stern-faced groups of mounted *Guardia Civil,* with guns and pistols ready at hand.

The steady tramp of marching feet is heard, and down the street parades a rabble of thousands, waving red banners and shouting songs of freedom, with frequent sinister cries of, *"A muerte Maura"* (Death to Maura), the Prime Minister, whom the people believe responsible for the death of Ferrer, the revolutionist.

May Day has brought all Madrid's discontented workmen, from factory, shop, and mill, into the streets, where they form an excitable, restless mob, needing only a spark to light the ever smoldering fire. In this city of gilded monarchy, "rouged anarchy" is never far away, and at any moment the red beast may come from out his hiding place. So Madrid is prepared and alert, never forgetting that other day in May, not so very many years ago, when the King and his Queen of an hour, while slowly driving toward their future palace home, in the magnificent carriage of tortoise shell drawn by eight snow-white horses, were almost touched by Death.

Out of one of the balconies fell a huge bouquet, not unlike the thousands of others that had been showered from every window all the way from the church. But from this one as it struck the earth there came a blinding flash, a fearful crash, and a cloud of smoke, that on clearing away showed a shattered coach, bleeding horses, and mutilated men lying on a bloody pavement. Except that the wedding gown of the Queen was splashed with red, neither she nor the King was harmed. With enviable calmness they burrowed their way out of the wreckage, getting into the carriage immediately behind, the one that had brought Princess Victoria to the church, and, as if nothing had happened, proceeded to the palace. But no sooner had they arrived than the King hurried away to the hospital to visit his wounded and dying escort, and then with splendid bravery walked along through the panic-stricken throngs in the crowded Puerta del Sol, seeking to restore confidence.

La Dama Errante, that famous novel of Pio Baroja, was inspired by this attempt at assassination, an event that left an ineradicable impression upon Baroja, as he states in his preface, having personally known several of the actors in the tragedy. Baroja, one of the most interesting writers of modern Spain, represents more completely than any other, modern Spain's ideas and tendencies. He has woven this story around a certain Doctor Aracil and his daughter Maria, whose characters are minutely outlined. Maria is brought up with aunts of whom he says, "The actual life of the Spanish woman is really sad. Without carnality and without romanticism, religion converted into a custom, the idea of the eternity of love lost, there remains to the Spanish woman no spiritual support. And then the casuistry of the Catholic education has inoculated them with a subtle hypocrisy; with the idea of finding themselves justified in all, if they arrive in good condition at the legal prostitution of matrimony. The habit of dissimulating and lying, and of going from time to time to the confessional, to wash away their little spiritual scabs, in company with a rustic, with an intense glance and a blue-black beard, gradually corrupted their souls."

The doctor is painted with rather vague, though somewhat extreme, views concerning the reformation of society, which, publicly expressed, bring him into touch with Nilo Brull, a Catalonian anarchist who, in the course of the narrative, tries to assassinate Alfonso the Thirteenth. Aracil, because of his acquaintance with Brull, falls under suspicion. He is forced to flee from Madrid across the border to Portugal, permitting many exquisite word pictures of this long muleback journey through little-known country. In reality, the book is a discussion of anarchism, its egotism under the guise of altruism, its inconsistencies, and its contradictions.

Nilo Brull, in a letter addressed to the public just before committing suicide, expresses the inordinate self-conceit of his type. He writes: "A few moments before dying, with the knowledge of my superiority over yourselves, I wish to speak to you.

"During all my life Society has pursued me, trapped me as if I had been a ferocious beast; being the best, I have been considered the worst; being first, they considered me as last.

"I would give my reasons for this altruistic work of mine if the Spaniards could understand me; but I am sure they will not understand—they cannot understand. Slaves do not understand rebellion, and you are slaves, all slaves, some of the King, others of morality, others of the military, others of God. Everything is slavery.

"I alone am rebellion. I am higher than Justice. My plan was, push the world toward chaos. I realized my Big Work alone. If I had had the necessity of an accomplice, I would never have reached the end. In Spain there is no man with enough heart to help me. There are not two like me. I am a lion in the midst of a yard full of hens. I believe that few men would have had my serenity. In the terrible moment, when I was on the balcony with the bomb in my hand, I saw in the street a few young girls who were laughing. None the less I did not hesitate. Pitiless as destiny, I condemned them beforehand to death. It was necessary.

"And when I had thrown it, surrounded by flowers! When it burst, I thought that it was tearing my entrails.

"Something similar must a woman feel giving birth to a child. I had given something alive to the world.

"Before me in Spain there was nothing. Nothing! After my great Act an Idea was living. I believe that my act is the biggest of its kind that has been committed. All Spaniards, if they were not idiots, should be grateful to me— all of them; the King, because I dignified his position; the aristocracy, because in front of peril they seemed to be less selfish than usual;

the people, because from me they learned the most effective form of protest.

"I am going to sink into unconsciousness by means of a bullet in my heart. Destroy my brains, blow them out! That would seem to me a sacrilege, and more, for then the doctors could not study them, and they will not find many like mine."

Doctor Aracil is the dilettante of anarchism; in love with his own rhetoric, delighting in such phrases as, "a dynamiter is something of an artist, a sculptor who, barbarous and cruel, molds with human flesh." Actually his rebellion goes no farther than opposition to what he considers antiquated customs and forms, being specially indignant, says Baroja, at the absurdities of modern letter writing. To us, the perhaps somewhat stilted politeness demanded by custom even between men in ordinary written intercourse is not absurd, but rather an interesting curiosity. Nothing could be more graceful than their mode of speech, the very construction of the language conducive to courtesy. A letter must be begun, *"Muy señor mío y distinguido señor,"* literally "My very great Lord and distinguished Sir"; winding up with, *"Su seguro servidor que besa su mano,"* which the American typewriter, with un-Spanish regard for time, clicks off into S.S.S. Q.B.S.M.—meaning, "Your constant servant who kisses your hand." If the letter be to a woman, for some unexplained reason you go to the other extreme, epistolarily throwing yourself at her feet, *"Que sus pies besa."* Should you be fortunate enough to know and write to any provincial presidents, civil governors, or equally important personages, the beginning of your letter will be: *"Excelentísimo señor don"*—"Most illustrious Lord Mr. ———."

And this oriental politeness is carried out in practice as well. If, as strangers, you rent a house or apartment in some one of the smaller cities, all the immediate neighborhood flocks to welcome you, saying as they leave: "You are very sympathetic to me. Remember, as long as you are here, that at number nine—or number fifteen or third-floor apartment (as the case may be)—you have a home and a friend."

How charming a courtesy, flattering and pleasing, whether heartfelt or not.

But to return to anarchism and the principles of government. With many a Spanish acquaintance in various parts of the country we discussed political questions, and, while naturally at variance in detail, everyone agreed that Spanish politics are about the most involved and complicated of those of any nation in the world; the most difficult to understand and follow, even for the Spaniards themselves.

Since the Restoration there are supposed to be two historical parties, Conservatives and Liberals, differing to great extent in name only, and neither apparently with any clearly defined program. Canovas, the original great leader of the Conservatives, a man of strong character and intelligence, claimed that his party was in reality Liberal, because its main work was the mainte‑ nance of the laws promulgated by the Liberal party, but never applied by them.

Segasta, the old head of the Liberals, more shrewd than Canovas, though not so talented, created the popular suffrage and labor laws, while allowing the everyday problems, so far as possible, to solve themselves. His political se‑ cret, according to gossip, was to trust to time and the death of somebody to settle them.

The Conservative party, ruling at this writing under Sanchez Guerra, is divided into several sharply antagonistic branches, with Maura, Cierva, and Toca as leaders; Guerra's immedi‑

257

ate following being only 180 out of the 405 in Congress.

The Liberals are likewise divided into distinct groups of thirty and forty deputies each; while there is also a Communist, a Socialist, and a Republican party.

But the politician rarely represents the public, for in spite of suffrage, he is appointed, rather than elected, gathering around the husbands, sons, brothers, cousins, and nephews of some twenty or thirty powerful families who form the governmental Center.

In addition to these various views and parliamentary grouping, public opinion is roughly separated into Right and Left. The Rights are fanatical obstructionists, inimical to anything that spells progress; the Lefts, representing the mass of the working people, are led by the great commercial centers such as Barcelona, Bilboa, and Valencia, where there exists a strong syndicalism, capable of causing trouble and disturbance at almost any time.

One friend sums up the whole matter by saying that Spanish politics resembles a weathercock in a twenty-knot breeze, the changes in government being not less than one a year—each beautifully variegated.

All of which bewildering confusion was foretold by legend and history, as related by the clever author of *The Diary of an Idle Woman.* "One day *le bon Dieu* rose in good humor as to creation in general, and especially as to this earthly planet. So He called together the patron saint of every country in order to confer some favor upon each.

"First appeared Saint George, glistening in silver armor, feathers, helmet, dragon and lance complete and stands before Him. 'What do you desire for your land?' asks *le bon Dieu.* 'Speak! It is possible I may grant it.'

" 'I want,' replied Saint George reverently, 'the finest navy in the world.'

" 'Granted,' says *le bon Dieu;* upon which Saint George collects his *mise en scène* and retires.

"Next comes Saint Louis, eldest son of the Church and of undoubted sanctity.

" 'What do you ask for France?' is the question; upon which Saint Louis, kneeling—which fiery Saint George forgot to do—answers, 'The bravest army that ever marched to battle.'

" 'Granted' is the reply; upon which exit Saint Louis to make way for Saint Joseph, Patron of Italy, who, in reply to the same question, expresses—with courtesy proper to his nation—his wish to possess 'the Empire of Art.'

"Saint Patrick asks for Ireland that no poisonous serpent or reptile shall ever trouble the soil.

" 'Granted, granted,' cries *le bon Dieu,* dismissing the martyred saints with a kindly nod. But suddenly he remembers that one guardian saint is missing. 'Where,' he demands, 'is that lazy Spaniard, Saint James? What a fellow that is, always putting off everything to mañana! Where is Santiago?'

"Suddenly a great noise is heard, of horses' hoofs clattering through the courts of Heaven, for Saint James being always late, invariably travels on horseback—and the patron saint of Spain gallops in.

"What does my good Saint James want?' asked *le bon Dieu,* smiling at the haste with which the saint precipitates himself from his saddle and hastens toward the throne.

" 'I desire,' cries Saint James, prostrating himself on the clouds (for of course all this takes place in Heaven, and Saint James is the most devoted of all the patron saints which rule over Europe), 'for my beloved Spain that we should be the wittiest of nations.'

" 'Granted.'

" 'And,' adds Saint James, seeing that *le bon Dieu* is in the best of tempers, 'that our women should be the most beautiful.'

" 'Hum, hum! Too much for one nation; nevertheless, for your sake, Santiago, who are such a good and pious knight, I will say granted for wit and beauty.' Upon which Saint James, rising and making a series of the most profound obeisances, was about to depart when he suddenly stopped and turned around. 'I forgot to say I also wanted to ask for the best government.'

" 'Now this is too much,' exclaimed *le bon Dieu,* exasperated at his urgency. 'To all the other saints I have only granted one wish, you already have two. To punish you, I declare that Spain shall never have any government at all.' "

Dos de Mayo is a day sacred to all Spaniards; for in 1808, on the second of May, after Charles the Fourth had left Madrid, lured to France by Napoleon, Spain was left abandoned and disrupted, apparently an easy prey to the hundred thousand Frenchmen who were then insolently swaggering through their country. An unarmed mob, in ungovernable fury, they flung themselves upon the French Imperial guard, who, in murderous retaliation, not only slaughtered the miserable rabble, but seized hundreds of other men, as well as women and children, forced them to kneel wherever taken, and shot them point blank. If you could only see Goya's picture of that massacre, you would understand the horror my words fail to express. Under a somber sky, within the light of a single smoking lantern, lie heaps of dead and dying. Some of the victims are throwing themselves before the gun muzzles in a spirit of supreme exaltation; others shrink back terrified, with faces drawn and haggard, or with hands before their eyes to shut out the approach of death. It is a page from Poe, so vividly portrayed that one can almost hear the cries of those in their last agony; can almost smell the blood that flows and flows until the ground shrieks with red.

But Spain's critical need, as so often happens, produced those leaders of men whose names are venerated to-day—Velarde and Daoiz, two young captains of artillery, who pleaded so earnestly with the men of Madrid to take up arms and fight against the foreign foe, that they succeeded in undamming the pent-up fury of a long-suffering people. They gave their lives in patriotic sacrifice, though not in vain, for they fired the first gun in the War of Independence, which expelled the French King and gave back Spain to the Spaniards.

So it is that the troops are gathering today in the Plaza de la Lealtad (loyalty) where stands the obelisk consecrated to these martyrs of liberty. A regiment of Lancers, with pennoned lances held rigidly in hand, encircle the square, which soon becomes a glittering mass of helmets and swords, and noisy with the blare of trumpets. But within the iron railing surrounding the monument there is the quiet of a church, and against the flower-banked monolith we see a field altar made ready for mass. Here are assembled students from the military and naval colleges, old war pensioners, decrepit and feeble as veterans should be, and all the living relatives of the massacred dead. Listen, and you will hear the royal march. Then between the raised swords of artillerymen, who have formed two lines from the entrance gate to the altar, comes the King, followed by a glittering file of generals, staff officers, and princes of the Church. Once they are seated, the Papal Nuncio celebrates that grandest of all religious functions— a military mass. During this, a solemn procession of soldiers marches by in salute to the monument. A splendid spectacle it is,—though all one seems to see are the tattered flags, red with the blood of Independence; all one hears are the funeral notes of the trumpets, long sustained and very sad—in memory of Spain's brave dead.

May 8

Madrid with its parks, its gardens, and many green places is like some emerald oasis in the midst of an almost treeless, wind-swept desert, open to every "embrace of the God of winds." Rising over two thousand feet above the sea, nearer heaven, geographically, than any other capital of the world, it gives point to the proverb that the throne of Spain is first after that of God.

It was the gouty toe of Charles the Fifth, however, that actually brought Madrid into its first prominence, for only in its keen mountain air could he obtain relief from pain. But its real sponsor was his eccentric, bigoted son, Philip the Second, who, finding the gloominess and bleak desolation of early-day Madrid congenial and to his liking, proclaimed it the capital of Spain for all time to come. There he lived until the city became unseemly gay—when he moved to the even more gloomy walls of the Escorial.

The home of Ferdinand, though not the same

palace as now exists, stood on exactly the same ground, directly above the little river Manzanares, which old writers quaintly describe as "not very good perfume for the nose." The present-day building is imposing—in size if not in beauty—an enormous mass poised on the edge of a cliff, overlooking a vast stretch of royal land. It offers a glorious view from the upper windows, the same view that framed the background of so many of Velásquez's pictures, a green valley that descends step by step to the gardens and parks,—famous in De Vega's comedies,—crossing the river in a succession of wooded reaches that finally join the far-away mountains of Guadarrama, giving a sense of tremendous distance.

How many a sad-hearted queen must have leaned her forehead against these very window-panes, seeing on the vague horizon the picture of unfulfilled dreams!

The palace within is magnificent in the usual princely fashion of Spain—a splendor that may perhaps be more easily grasped if reduced to a dollar formula. The throne room, for example, with its sparkling rock-crystal chandeliers mounted in silver, its gorgeous frescoes and art treasures, is alone estimated to have cost nearly a million dollars. While many other rooms are of almost equal richness, some are of much greater artistic value, their ceilings and walls of porcelain, gold-bronzed and mirrored, or decorated with rare marbles and hung with priceless Flemish tapestries—the greatest collection in number and beauty of any court in Europe.

We have wandered through all these rooms, alone, except for an attendant, but we have also stood in the wide galleries that encircle the great courtyard, when it was filled with a brilliant company awaiting the passing of royalty. Impressively, the procession wound its way through carpeted corridors to the solemn strains of a march by Maestro Pares. It entered the palace chapel, and there Ascension Day mass was celebrated with all its accustomed grandeur. Only those in procession supposedly take part in this ceremonial service, but under the guidance of the King's secretary we were led by a private entrance through the sacristy into the personal tribune of the Marques de Torrecilla, which is very like one of those *intime* boxes of a French theater. From behind a glassed front we look down upon a mise en scène of glittering splendor; for, in spite of the gorgeously vested priests massed about the altar, in spite of the inspiring

Misa of Merlier, we are left with the impression of some perfectly rehearsed pageant, as one by one, in perfect order, the picturesque figures file into place. His Majesty the King, wearing the Knighthood order of the Golden Fleece, proceeds to a white-satin-canopied dais embroidered with gold and silver, just at the left of the altar. Below him, on tapestry-covered benches, sit the Infantes and Infantas. On the opposite side, the grandees of Spain, in the medieval uniform of the several brotherhoods of chivalry, take their places. Behind them are ranged the chief functionaries of the court and the army, dazzling with ribboned decorations. With all the pomp of the most famous court in Europe, the service proceeds, ending with "El Andante" of Eschaikonsky, one of those sorrowful Russian laments wherein seems to wail the soul of Slavonia, so tender and pathetic that the heart is long time saddened.

Later we watch the medieval change of Household Guard as, to the music of Arab *chirivias,* the Halberdiers, in archaic costume and carrying fifteenth-century halberds—long staffs with battle-ax and pike at the end—come swinging down the street, to mount with strangely pompous step the grand stairway of black and

267

white marble. Two by two they relieve the sentinels before the doors of the royal apartments, watched day and night. Then from the palace balcony we look down upon the pretty maneuvers of mounting the outdoor guard, when the infantry in intricate formation parade about the inner palace yard, keeping time with Germany's goose step to the Royal March of Spain—Germany's music, written for Frederick the Great, as a march for his giant grenadiers.

These and many other charming courtesies we owe to the King's personal secretary, who, despite a thousand duties and countless calls upon his day, found the time to act as cicerone and counselor. No trouble was ever too great, nothing was left undone in his effort to please. All he asked was that we hold his country in pleasant remembrance; more than content if, thanks to him, the strangers speak well of his beloved Spain and do not in ignorance ridicule customs and habits which, because different from ours, might seem open to gibes. Public opinion as we gather it agrees in believing that the greater number of those who fill high places in the palace are inferior in mind to the King himself, and as a rule as unsympathetic as His Majesty is *simpatico;* the one exception in that opinion seems to be *Don Emilio de Torres, secratario particular de S. M. el Rey,* a modest gentleman who has won the rarest of all prizes in Spain, universal public esteem. In this respect he is following in the footsteps of his royal master, Alfonso the Thirteenth, who, without question, is the most popular reigning monarch in the world.

In spite of the dubious privilege of being the thirteenth of his name and, when born, of being placed under the protecting influence of the Holy Father, Pope Leo the Thirteenth, Alfonso seems to be blessed with his full share of this world's best gifts. The Fates certainly have endowed him with a most interesting personality, with an enthusiasm that never seems to wane, with a courage that knows no fear, indubitably proven during the anarchistic riots in Barcelona. And it is no exaggeration to state that perhaps his sense of humor, his gayety, and his good-fellowship have done as much as anything else to keep the crown steady during these days of universally wabbling coronets.

Even the most ardent republican of Spain admits a sneaking fondness for Alfonso. A well-authenticated story tells that this man, after a

fiery speech of most extreme views, was called
to the palace and good-naturedly warned by the
king to this effect, "If you succeed in overthrow-
ing the monarchy, I shall run for first president."
And, without a question, Alfonso would win.

It is at a polo match, played on the King's
private grounds, to which admission is had only
by the King's personal invitation, that we see
Alfonso most intimately. Outside the players,
there were not more than fifty present—all Spaniards but ourselves, among whom were the
stately Queen Mother; that most amiable lady,
the Infanta Isabel, the King's aunt; the Infantes Don Alfonso and Don Ferdinand; the
Duque and Duquesa of Alba; the Marqueses of
Viana and Torrecilla; and others of the King's
familiars. Riding up to the clubhouse, for the
King plays and plays well, he dismounted, coming first to us, as strangers, bidding us welcome
with that simple courtesy which in Spain belongs to commoner and prince alike. His first
understanding words mark him as, not only a
splendid king, but a great gentleman, with whom
one might be quite as natural as with anyone
whom one respects. And later, when the Queen
Mother bade us to afternoon tea, a brew which

A STREET IN MADRID

AIRPLANE VIEW OF MADRID, THE ROYAL PALACE IN THE CENTER.

gossip says until the advent of the English Queen was sold as medicine, we find the same charming simplicity, a simplicity only to be found among those whose position has not to be established. The Queen Mother, María Cristina, may perhaps never entirely lose her air of queenship, but above everything else she is a mother who, to defend the throne for her then unborn son, brought to bear an invincible power, mightier than all the guns of Europe—a great love and an absolute devotion, still lavished upon the man-son with an adoration beautiful to see.

May 9

The heart of Madrid beats at the Puerta del Sol, that axle of a wheel from which, like so many spokes, the streets radiate in every direction. And on whatever street of the city you may happen to be, you need but to look for the building numbered one, to find yourself within that center of the city's life—a plaza where all day long and much of the night there is a perfect sea of heads, plowed by crossing lines of carriages and automobiles traveling at a crawl. It is a place of restless idleness, of a feverish eagerness for doing anything, which is generally nothing; the dawdling ground for the unem-

271

ployed; the hunting ground for beggars and co-
cottes, eternally questioning with their eyes the
young idlers and the old libertines. It is the
tryst for lovers; the meeting place for friends;
the rendezvous for those who wish to spend
money or for those seeking to steal it. It is a
human hive of linked luxury and squalor. A
shadeless, treeless, flowerless bedlam of noise.

And scarcely more than ten minutes away, you
may walk in the broad "greenery of the Prado,"
—meadow is its English name,—once a famous
promenade, but now still more famous as the
site of the Museo del Prado, one of the world's
picture kingdoms, whose sovereigns are the im-
mortals: Titian, Velásquez, El Greco, Ribera,
Murillo, Goya. Here Goya shows himself at
his best or his worst, according to varying opinion, at the very entrance of the main gallery,
where side by side hang those oft-photographed
and much-discussed "Maja Vestida" and "Maja
Desnuda."

The wide corridors of this museum show long
vista after vista of world masterpieces, a glorious rainbow of heavenly color. You see Titian
in the "Wisdom of Age," seventy years old,
when he painted the finest equestrian portrait
in the world, that of Charles the Fifth. You see

him in the lustful vigor of young manhood with his "Bacchanal" of sensual charm. You see him as an obsequious courtier in "La Gloria," the only worldly possession the flattered King took to Yuste Monastery when he resigned the throne; the last object looked upon by his dying eyes.

Here is the greater part of the work of the greatest painter of Spain—Velásquez, who has left pages and pages of revealing court history, a gallery in realism of ugly dwarfs, cringing beggars, bestial drunkards, as well as magnificent warriors, martyrs, kings, and queens—all just as his eyes saw them, with uncompromising fidelity,

It is also the home of the surgeon artist Ribera, who with paint and brush dissects the human body, giving us ghastly exhibits of emaciated saints and livid carcasses, green with the hue of decay. Drawing each muscle, outlining every wrinkle, he emphasizes all the repulsive ills of the flesh in black shades and yellow lights, splendid in their somberness and savagery.

Then Murillo, that master of Christian art, visualizes the dream of the Holy Catholic Church. His Virgins are purer than purity. With hands devoutly clasped, eyes wide open in adoration, they seem to have been taken into the very presence of God. Every canvas carries a feeling of gladness, of peace, and of consolation.

And finally there is El Greco's astonishing series of portraits, a constant strife for originality rather than for beauty, every picture showing his own unmatched haunting conception and color.

But to see all we needs must linger here for weeks; to tell all would require an entire book and a far, far more practiced pen than mine. So I am carrying you away on a little visit to the only two-storied streets thus far passed by in Madrid's feverish rush to modernize. They serve to illustrate Spain's universal fondness for the naïve tales of childhood. One is the Calle de las dos Hermanas, so named when nearly half of Spain was yet in the hands of the Arabs.

In those far-away days there lived in one of the fortress-like houses a widowed nobleman and his two daughters, whom he often had to leave in charge of servants when he was called away to fight in the constant wars against the Moorish invader. Seeing these two sisters alone and unprotected save for the women of the household, the young gallants of the neighborhood became so audaciously insistent in their attentions that the elder of the two conceived the idea of dressing as a man, the better to safeguard their honor. The ruse succeeded so well that one of the love swains, angry at his own repulse, determined to revenge himself and sent word to the absent father that almost every night a young man could be seen entering his house and not leaving until the following morning.

Upon receiving the news the father returned in all haste, concealing himself within his own house, that he might see all who should come in. At nightfall the elder daughter, disguised as usual, entered the house, going directly to her sister's room to allay any possible anxiety on her part. The father, now convinced of the intruder's dishonor, followed closely after the supposed lover, and on finding the two sisters in close embrace, blinded by rage, stabbed them to death. From which time the tragic street has been known to all Madrid as the "Street of the Two Sisters."

Tucked away in another corner is La Calle de la Cabeza,—the street of the head,—in which lived two youths, Ruiz and Medina, both enamored of the same fair one. Ruiz was diffident about declaring his love, but Medina, accustomed to such adventure—for he had been a soldier in Flanders—made love so boldly and pleaded so humbly that the lady consented to become his wife. The marriage was celebrated with all the quaint ceremony of the time, the bride and groom receiving the adieus of the wedding guests from the balcony of the nuptial chamber. Hardly were they left alone when they heard shouts, the clash of swords, and a loud cry for help. Medina rushed out, only to be killed by a treacherous dagger thrust, which left him lifeless at the foot of the crucifix that stood in the center of the street.

The bride of an hour, nearly insane with grief, fell desperately ill. During all her long sickness, Ruiz was ever by her side, trying to efface from her memory the horrible tragedy, hoping that in time she would turn to him for happiness. As he had planned, so it happened, and again there was a wedding feast prepared, for which Ruiz went to the *rastro* to buy his favorite dish, a calf's head to roast, concealing it under his cloak. To reach home by the shorter way, he had to pass the image of Christ, which he had not approached since the death of his friend Medina. As he neared the foot of the crucifix, two guardians of the peace happened to see drops of blood falling from beneath his cape, and they asked Ruiz what he was carrying.

Opening his cloak, he saw the eyes of his friend looking at him in reproach. Horrified, he tried to drop the accursed head, but could not for the long hairs wound themselves about his fingers like serpents and held them fast. In a panic of fear, there before the crucifix, he confessed his crime, the murder of Medina, the unfortunate husband of the lady he was to marry that night.

May 14

In modernized, cosmopolitan Madrid, pure, undiluted Spain is rarely found except at some such bullfight as we saw this afternoon, when torrents of vehicles stream down the main streets, between dense lines of foot passengers. Drivers of huge, lumbering omnibuses crack their whips in invitation to the walking throng. Speeding motor cars, with warning honk, shoot by ramshackle cabs that are rattling along to the sound of jingling bells. Every social class is represented; every sort and description of wheeled conveyance is in use. A motley crowd, all hurrying in one direction.

With the others we fight our way through the entrance into the Plaza de Toros. No crowd is more picturesque than a Spanish crowd. Certainly the setting of a bullfight is wonderful: a

huge amphitheater with no roof but the blue of
the sky; an immense circular expanse of golden
sand, that the bloody fight will soon purple with
sickening splashes; tiers upon tiers of seats,
sown with bright tones of mottled color, like a
terraced garden. All around, in spacious loges,
sit the señoras and señoritas of the aristocratic
world, wearing white mantillas held in place by
crimson carnations that press forward curly
locks of black, black hair. They lean over the
edge of the boxes, full of expectation, their
shapely white arms lying across gorgeous man-
teaus that on entering they had spread over the
front railing. Shawls of blue, black shawls, red
shawls, white shawls, purple shawls, green
shawls, all heavily embroidered in floral design,
all deeply fringed—a splendid hedge of exotic
flowers. The great crowd awaits, nervously impatient, throbbing with excitement, like some
troubled sea that lies half in shadow, half in the
glittering sunlight that beats down with burning rays. The stage is set.

Then comes a trumpet call. A splendid procession enters the arena, led by two mounted
alguaciles—marshals of the bull ring—dressed
in black velvet, with plumed hats and short capes
such as were worn in the time of Philip the

Third. Three matadors walk in front, the eldest in the center, a dazzling array, all pink-stockinged, their feet encased in jewel-buckled pumps. They wear knee breeches of silk, with broad gilt embroidery up the seam; fine lawn shirts, delicate as a woman's garment, down which hangs a narrow red scarf meeting an equally vivid waist sash of red; a jacket heavy with golden flowers, epauleted with long tassels of the same glittering metal; and a princely cloak of colored satin, folded over the arm. As they advance in the swaying motion ordained by the convention of centuries, with a somewhat dainty, mincing step, they look, in these ballroom costumes that show even filmy lace handkerchiefs peeping out of gold-woven pockets, as though ready for a dance—and so they are, even though the dance may be a ballet of death.

Behind each matador comes his own troup or *cuadrilla — capeadores* and *banderilleros —* equally spangled, fringed, and filigreed,—but with silver instead of gold; then the *picadors,* with wide-brimmed cockaded sombreros, skin breeches lined with protecting strips of steel, and sparkling jackets, astride ill-fated nags with one eye bandaged and mercifully drugged. Lastly, driven by *chulos*—the camp followers of this little army—are teams of mules afire with color, their harness gayly covered with tassels and worsted balls, flying at bridle top little national flags.

To the blare of martial music this dazzling *paseo*, slowly and with great dignity, moves toward the royal box, today occupied by the Mayor of Madrid. He receives them standing, and to their salute and deep bows, like some Roman Emperor of old, he gives the signal for this red battle to begin, throwing to the leading *alguacil* the key which is to unlock the dark cell, where for fifteen hours the bulls have been bellowing and fretting for the light and food denied them all that time.

A second trumpet call, and the arena clears—except for the *capeadores* and the *picadors,* who range themselves against the high wooden barrier that encircles the rim for protection. The *toril* door opens. A savage bull flashes forward. As he plunges into the light, a colored rosette, the herd badge, is jabbed into his shoulder, further infuriating him. A magnificent stage entrance.

The bull stops short, stunned at the shouts of ten thousand voices. Then he sees the hated red, the glittering figures of the *picadors* with their threatening spears. Lowering his horns, he rushes blindly at the nearest animal. Despite the courage and strength of the *picador,* who drives a long, iron-piked pole between his shoulders, to hold him off, the powerful brute reaches him, boring his horns into the luckless horse, dragging out his entrails and throwing the man against the railing with a resounding crash. A *capeador* rushes forward, deftly drawing the bull away with his brilliant-colored *capa* that he flings into the animal's face, allowing the *chulos* time to lift the *picador* to his feet, his clothes so heavily padded with steel that he cannot rise alone. There is a hush of breathless excitement, as on the *capeador's* skill and quickness depends the life of the prostrate man.

Another *picador* rides up with menacing spear. This one a perfect horseman, and of amazing strength, holds the bull at bay. The arena rings with the frantic applause of a people inflamed by a horrible enthusiasm.

A third *picador* is unhorsed, and the poor riderless beast, fearfully torn and wounded to death, staggers wildly about the ring. Another writhes in agony on the sand as the bull furiously attacks the miserable carcass, until it is put out of misery by a quick dagger thrust from

281

a *chulo* who creeps up from behind. The smell of blood is strong in the nostrils, almost overpowering, when the trumpet again sounds.

Now the *banderilleros* play their part, which is to further enrage the already furious animal. These graceful, agile figures in colored satin and silvery embroidery, with *banderillas*—wooden sticks, carrying a large fishhook at one end, and covered with colored paper, gayly beribboned—plant themselves in front of the bull. They stamp their feet and jeer, to excite the animal to attack and he anxiously paws the ground in anger, not knowing what this new torment means. Holding a *banderilla* in each uplifted hand, the man approaches nearer, when the bull drives down upon him, lowering his horns to gore. The man receives him at full charge, rising on tiptoe and leaning far forward, fixing the dart into each side of the neck, dexterously leaping aside just in time to avoid the fearful horns —a jumping flash of color.

Breathlessly the public follows every shifting change. They know every detail of the game and are ready with approving shouts if the darts are rightly and fearlessly placed, or equally ready with groans and hisses for any stupidity or seeming cowardice.

Twice, three times, this is done, and then everything is in readiness for the dangerous climax—the *suerte de matar*.

The matador, until now a spectator, takes from a waiting attendant a *muleta*—a little stick from which hangs down a red cloth, like a flag, concealing a long, dagger-like sword. He goes over to the royal box, asking permission to deal the death blow. Then, in a few inaudible words, he dedicates the killing to some sainted lady, and walks out toward the bull—alone—his life in his hands.

A perfect silence. All eyes are fixed on those two, face to face in the middle of a vast arena, a splendid figure in gold, quiet and self-possessed, an infuriated bull with blood streaming down his flanks from the slashes of the *picadors'* lances and the barbed darts of the *banderilleros*.

The man plays with the bull, seems to hypnotize him. He flirts the maddening color of his *muleta* before the animal's face in tormenting and bewildering passes. At length the enormous brute, bellowing with rage, rushes upon him. The matador scarcely moves from his place, drawing the bull from one side to the other with a skillful motion of the red cloth, allowing him to lumber by, just grazing his arm, so close as

283

to dim the golden epaulets with rage-foaming saliva. Again and again the animal charges with hot fury this hectoring enemy whom he never seems to reach. The matador is expertly maneuvering to bring the bull with his forelegs close together, in the position required for giving the successful death stroke that has to be placed in a tiny three-inch space near the shoulder blade.

Sixteen thousand spectators are looking with ardent eyes, thrilled with emotion as the horns time and again brush against the spangled costume.

At last everything seems propitious, and Granero, the idol of the people, draws his delicate sword from beneath the *muleta,* raises it to the height of his eyes, takes careful aim, and flings himself between the horns, lowered for attack. Man and beast are a confused mass.

Who has conquered? Contrary to the usual animal instinct upon which the fighters base their strategy, the bull, christened with frightful irony, "Pocapena," Little Trouble, has unexpectedly raised his head. Impaling the tall, glittering figure, he lifts it aloft, shakes it for a few seconds, as a child might a discarded doll, and then tosses it brutally against the barrier, where, with a last shiver, the body lies motionless. Another gladiator victim to the blood lust of the arena.

Two hours later intimate friends cut off Granero's *coleta,* that knot of plaited hair, the sign of the bullfighter, looked upon as almost semisacred and never removed until death or retirement. The last curtain call has been rung.

11

Old and New Castile

May 20

The road to Royalty's city of eternal sleep—
the Escorial—is like the path to that "bourne
from which no man returns," short and swift.
Little more than half an hour from Madrid and
we catch sight of a grim, gray pile of granite,
cut from the savage rock mass of the mountain, a
mountain in itself, lying on the lap of a mountain, whose color and ruggedness it absorbs.
Colossal, cold, and austere, it moodily broods
over one of the most somber sites of somber Castile, amid a bleak heap of ore rubbish—*escoria*.
A splendid background, these mountains, for
this monument erected in the image of its master; expressing perfectly in stone the morbid,
melancholy soul of a king to whom sunshine and
gayety were anathema.

Charles the Fifth during his lifetime had
often signified a desire to have a fitting burial
place for himself and his descendants, and
Philip, his son, after several years' search decided upon this wild, secluded slope of the Gua-

286

darrama. The building was dedicated to Saint Lawrence, his patron saint. According to an old story, when siege was laid to the city of San Quentin, the commander in chief was forced to direct his cannon fire against the church of Saint Lawrence, to the great damage of that building. Philip, fanatically superstitious, was afraid that the saint might take revenge for having treated his home so badly, so he made a vow that he would build another richer and greater church than the one he had ruined, and dedicate it to the saint. Consequently, in his plans for the Escorial, he insisted that the architect should arrange the monastery-palace in the form of a gridiron, the symbol of Saint Lawrence. And there is no denying this arrangement, however historians may gibe at what they term a pretty legend. The four square towers with pointed steeples certainly represent the inverted legs of the gridiron upon which the martyr saint was burned. The church and the palace, projecting to one side, form the handle, while the internal courts and cloisters, running at absolute right angles, make the intersecting bars.

In this grandiose building Philip reserved for himself but a tiny corner, severely plain, poorly furnished; for, according to his own statement, he wanted nothing more than a cell in which he might bear his weary limbs to the grave. Here, close to the nave of the church, this royal recluse in the "pride of humbleness" secreted himself, embracing solitude as a lover would his bride.

The bedroom of the King is a veritable monastery cell, with no light except from the adjoining study. A couch is sunk in the shadows of the farthest corner. Over it a window opens directly opposite the high altar. Without moving, Philip could follow the celebration of mass, to which, at the break of day, he was awakened by the chant of monks. Here he died after fourteen years of seclusion, his hands clinging to the same cross his father had held in the last hours of his life at Yuste, his eyes turned toward the Christ crucified, crowning the altar beyond. Through the little window we look out upon the same scene that held his dying gaze, almost feeling the presence of that grim specter, who, in his final agony broke the windowpane in a supreme effort to approach nearer to God.

There are, of course, royal apartments furnished with splendor, superbly decorated by Goya, and hung with magnificent tapestries. They are now a deserted waste of unoccupied rooms, never dwelt in; for, as cheery Alfonso the Thirteenth once laughingly remarked, all too soon the Escorial would be his everlasting dwelling place. Indeed, down in the black and gold vault, the pantheon of kings and the mothers of kings, directly beneath the high altar where masses and prayers for the dead are continuously intoned, there may be seen among the even rows of sarcophagi, all identical in size and all wrought in precisely the same elaborate pattern, three without inscriptions—awaiting the King, the Queen, and the Queen Mother.

Wander as long as you may through this palace of a thousand rooms, you will find little other than the dreariness of a tomb, with Death the only inhabitant.

From the adjacent village of Guadarrama begins the ascent of those beautiful strongholds of gray rock that separate new and old Castile. Today the summit is veiled in vaporous mists that cover the solitary height with a rose-tinted shawl, red-striped by the lazy sun, beneath which unrolls an ocean of space, without limit, except for the horizon. Within the clouds crouches a lion of stone, commemorating the opening of this aërial route built at the order of

Ferdinand the Sixth to reach Granja, the beloved home of his father.

Through great forests of pine, alongside deep ravines, the highway leaps to the plains and to the "Golden Cage," built to rival the splendor of the Court of Versailles. As we breathe in the sweet perfumes of its garden park, our first thought is expressed aloud: "It seems as though we were in Versailles." "In Versailles!" responds the attendant. "What can Versailles be beside this?"

It was Philip the Fifth, grandson of Louis the Fourteenth, who, by a lavish expenditure which, for a time, bled dry the purse of Spain, tried not only to equal but to eclipse the home of his youth. He was splendidly abetted by Elizabeth, his Queen, who, during the King's absence, built, as a surprise, the famous fountains which occasioned his historic remark, "Three millions of pesetas have brought me only three minutes of pleasure!" Almost enough to dampen the spirits of the most loving wife!

In whatever direction one goes, the song of water is insistently loud. On all sides sheets of falling spray glisten in the sun like fragments of a broken mirror, hurtling against the bronze allegorical figures centered in every pool. Before the palace, fountain succeeds fountain, gradually ascending the steep incline so that the water may trickle down among the flowers, leaping from stone to stone with a harmony of sound only possible from the hand of nature. On the heights are massed forests of dark evergreens, an incomparable background for the garden trees, now, with spring in their veins, so bubbling with happiness that in their joy they powder the air with butterfly blossoms.

Even as the Escorial bears the unmistakable imprint of the despondent Philip the Second, so Granja reflects Philip the Fifth, who could never forget France.

With regret we turn back through the leafy avenues of San Ildefonso toward Segovia.

May 24

In Segovia we find the Spain of our dreams— real Spain. A city that wears its well-patched cloak of antiquity with all the pride and hauteur of old Castile, conscious of noble birth and long lineage. There is, too, more than a touch of Spain's habitual melancholy, adding only another charm to this legendary city whose very birth is legendary, whose whole life is legendary, with scarcely a street or a building that does not possess its legend of faith, of heroism, of tragedy, or of love.

Majestically she reclines on a throne of stone that rises perpendicularly between the silvery Eresma and the noisy Clamores. The mingled waters bathe the prow of the rock—an arrow-headed point, carrying on its extreme tip a fortress castle thickly set with soaring spires and towers that give it the appearance of some splendid battleship bristling with fighting turrets. The very rock resembles a great wave petrified as the gallant ship thrusts the waters aside.

No other military citadel in all Spain has such singular beauty of location. It so follows the lines and the color of the precipice on which it stands, that it seems of natural growth, splendidly typifying the warlike religious spirit of the Middle Ages, an eternal emblem of Segovia's restless past.

We enter by a drawbridge across the moat wide and deep, and visit, one by one, the regal halls of lofty, raftered ceilings. It is recorded of the "room of the rope" that Alfonso the Wise, proud and arrogant in his astronomical knowledge and study of the heavens, one day expressed the heretical belief that the earth must revolve around the sun. A Franciscan friar severely reproved him, saying he talked as though he believed the Creator should have consulted him in forming the universe, to which Alfonso listened in contemptuous silence. But that very night a terrible storm arose. A lightning bolt struck the royal apartment, severely burning the King, and the tempest continued until Alfonso confessed his fault at the feet of the monk whom he had scorned. As a sign of sincere repentance, he ordered the cornice stone of this room to be carved with the insignia and rope of Saint Francis.

It is but a step to the gayeties of the shaded Plaza Mayor, surrounded by balconied houses, where a brass band is blaring the national airs. Under the arcaded walks, "glassing" themselves in shop windows, are cadets from the artillery school, a goodly-looking lot of youngsters, whose great ambition, apparently, is to appear as much like the King as possible.

From here we go through a crooked maze of streets, passing the singular Casa de los Picos, that bristles with pointed stones like an outraged porcupine preparing for battle,—one of the most pictured curiosities of Spain. Then we pass the ancient synagogue, long ago exorcised by holy water into a Christian convent. Behind its walls live and die an "enclosed" sisterhood, their only communication with the outside world being a small partitioned turntable inserted in the entrance door, which, while completely hiding the sisters from sight, allows them to hear and receive the petitions of the devotees kneeling without. How many times in the first shadows of the night those doors have listened to ardent prayers bathed in tears! Even now we see one slight veiled figure carrying a newborn child, her sorrow-laden voice reaching our ears. May her prayer be granted!

When at last we find ourselves within Segovia's busiest plaza, it sparkles with all the glitter of its quicksilver name—Azoquejo. Market day has littered it with little stalls. On the ground, in front, is a glorious rainbow medley of merchandise, which, together with the peasants, gay in bright aprons and gaudily handkerchiefed heads, pushing their way through the clutter, paint a perfect orgy of color.

Straight through this market square runs a colossal aqueduct, bringing water on its shoulders from far-away snowy heights, forced by the magical genius of Rome to vault across the distant valley and then, with gigantic strides, to climb Segovia's hill. Endless strings of patient

ROMAN AQUEDUCT AT SEGOVIA

PUERTA DEL ALCÁZAR

donkeys staggering under the heavy loads laid across their backs are continually winding in and out between the huge pillars that serve as frames for quaint pictures of lovely old balconied houses, or else to niche great patches of blue cut from the surrounding sky.

The only way to appreciate the magnitude of this Roman wonder is to lean up against one of the pillars. The lounging idlers watch us with baffled amazement as we measure our pygmy selves with the towering height, gaining a lasting respect for the audacity of those early Titans. It is striking enough by sunlight, but seen later under a hazy moon, it looked like some fantastic monster crouching in the hollow of the square, its hundred legs hardly visible against the darker shades of the city.

We feel ourselves carried back to fabled days and belief in the peasant story that shoulders the poor Devil with another love episode. But he is allowed to display so little imagination as to make to a Segovian beauty the identical proposition which he made to his victim of Tarragona, offering, in exchange for the promise of her hand, to build in one night a perfect bridge that would make unnecessary the daily wearying task of fetching water from the valley. Having plenty of "the first vice of the first woman," the Segovian maid consented, but when morning showed a seemingly perfect bridge, fickleness, that other womanly frailty, proved the stronger, and she repented, flying to her father confessor for help. He, obliging man, found a few stones still lacking at one end, and released the lady from her promise, from which time the Devil in disgust has kept away from Segovia.

As for that other Segovian beauty of storied fame, María Esther, the Jewess, around whom the Roman Church weaves a miracle drama, her tomb, seen this morning in the cloisters of the cathedral, proves at least that she herself was not a myth.

While time, of course, consecrates and beautifies, María del Salto must have been seductively beautiful to have made all the Christian maidens of her day so madly jealous that they spread abroad evil reports. The spiteful whispers in time turned to open accusations and finally led to her condemnation.

The narrative pictures her bound and helpless, being dragged down the steep, twisting road that swiftly descends into the valley like some dried-up torrent, pursued by a furious mob scourging and stoning her. In a half swoon, she stumbled

along this *via dolorosa,* down to the bottom of
the precipice, across the turbulent river, and
then up the sinister Peña Grajera (the cliff of
vultures), from whose top criminals were flung.
The spirit of this unhappy girl utterly failed her
when she saw death so near, and sinking to the
ground in despair of help from her Hebrew
gods, she called upon the Virgin, who immediately appeared, bringing her new courage and,
upholding her in her arms as she leaped from
the mountain top into the valley below, where
she alighted unhurt, in proof of complete innocence.

On the spot where María del Salto landed,
one of the most beautiful in the neighborhood
of Segovia, rises the Santuario de Fuencisla,
still sheltering the Virgin of miraculous rescues,
for the spiritual alleviation of spiritually minded
travelers.

May 26

One way out of this valley of poetry, a country of running waters, leads past the little
twelve-sided church of Vera Cruz, built by the
Knights Templar in imitation of the Holy Sepulcher at Jerusalem. It is as a shepherd watching his sheep. Although almost eight centuries

old, the sanctuary still retains the magic of its classic lines, seemingly as eternal as the ever changing distant clouds now drifting over the cold Sierras that lie outstretched the full length of the way into Avila.

Like Segovia, Avila is a city of war, preserving all the characteristics of the Middle Ages, which fortified her into a frontier stronghold against the devastating Moors. Both these "sister cities" cling to pedestals of rocks, gazing out upon a wide sweep of unruffled plain, encircled by rugged mountains. But in Avila, man, as well as nature, has encased the city in an imposing wall of stone, a wall defended by eighty-six towers so closely strung together as to cause them to be likened to a diadem of glowing topaz. They crown the granite hill and appear to center in the fortress cathedral, whose military-looking apse, embedded within the city's ramparts, projects so as to form the clasp of this golden circlet.

The castle-like cathedral is a true child of these warriors of austere faith whose fighting spirit is so clearly imprinted upon the almost windowless, massive gray building, with its entrance door guarded by two giant figures holding spiked war clubs. How perfect a setting for the militant prelates and the knights in coats of mail, who knelt amid bloodstained banners and rattling lances as mass was sung to the accompaniment of distant booming cannon.

The unrelenting cruelty of those early days is evidenced by the legendary reception given Saint Vincente and his sisters, Sabina and Cristeta, who sought in Avila refuge from the persecutions of the Romans. But the people of Avila, weary of strife and seeing in their coming a cause for further trouble, went out to meet them beyond the city walls. Here they were welcomed by having their heads mashed against a rock, and their poor bodies were left to rot by the roadside. No sooner had the people departed than an immense serpent wriggled out from a hole in the stone and coiled around the sainted corpses, on watchful guard.

Now it so happened, the ancient chronicle records, that a Jew, drawn thither by curiosity, approached too near, and the serpent, with angry hisses, wound about his neck, intending to kill him for the desecration. But on the point of being strangled, the Jew was heard to utter the word "Jesus," whereupon the serpent immediately released him. In gratitude the Hebrew caused this fine old Romanesque

building of San Vincente to be erected on the
spot where the stone stood and buried the saints
within a magnificent sarcophagus which remains as the chief glory of the church, even to
this day.

For many years the makers of any particu-
larly solemn oath were brought to San Vincente
and forced to thrust their hands into the hole in
the rock, which you may see today in the crypt
of this national monument, adjuring the serpent
to bite them if they swore falsely. But the
church put a ban on such uses when one of its
bishops came to swear to the truth of his episcopal utterances—and was bitten.

But in no such spirit of levity should one
rightfully approach this hermit city, still living
in medieval seclusion behind sheltering walls;
but rather in the mood of a pilgrim visiting
some holy shrine, for here in Avila was cradled
that exquisite mystic spirit which took earthly
form just inside the gateway known today as the
Puerta de Santa Theresa. When Saint Theresa
was a mere child her mother died, and, haunted
by visions of martyrdom even at that early age,
she sobbingly threw herself before a picture of
the Virgin, entreating the great Mother of all
to take her mother's place. From that time on,

she spent her life with her face upturned to heaven, and gradually her soul was transformed into a mirror in which the face of Christ was always reflected.

While she was still but a young girl, Theresa took the irrevocable black veil, and in "raptures" she often heard the voice of God comforting her, ever contending that faith illumined by the flame of heavenly love brought glimpses of what lay beyond the veil, even permitting a prevision of the days of after life. And who is there that dare deny this?

After years of strife and persecution Theresa was carried in a vision into the realms of heaven, where, a few years later, she became the "bride of Christ," taking his name—a mystery still celebrated in Avila every August.

When the time came for her death-bells to ring, Theresa is said to have opened her eyes just long enough to ask the reason for their ringing. "For Matins," was the answer. "Matins! I will sing them in heaven." And her eyes closed in a last sleep.

The room where she was born has been converted into a lovely little chapel where we and others who are more truly devout go to seek consolation.

Turning toward Salamanca, we take the path so often taken by the Catholic sovereigns when they rode under the picturesque Puerta del Alcázar, to mourn beside the superb monument where their only son, Prince John, lay buried. Dressed in sackcloth, Ferdinand and Isabella would seat themselves in the choir stalls above the tomb and sorrowfully gaze down for hours at a time upon the marble effigy of their beloved child, the pure upturned face wreathed in alabaster locks of rippling hair. A boy of uncommon promise he was, if history is to be believed, whose death changed the entire course of Spain's future.

But what bigots these monarchs were! As we leave the Monastery we see scattered about the courtyard of the castle palaces many of those stone pigs set up in mockery of the Jews who were so cruelly persecuted during all their reign.

They call Salamanca the "City of Learning," and in the far-away days when Gil Blas, astride his uncle's mule, left Oviedo to study at Salamanca, its university was one of the oldest and most celebrated in the world. It was the new Athens, to which flocked intellectuals from every country, outrivaling the other two "great queens of science"—Paris and Oxford. Its more than eight thousand students were all garbed in picturesque velvet cloaks, three-cornered hats, and small swords—as Cervantes graphically described. But year by year, little by little, its star has declined, until the number of students has fallen to fewer than three hundred.

Along one side of a sleepy little *plazuela* rises the richly chiseled university façade. It resembles some church missal of time-stained ivory grotesquely carved with an heraldic tree of life, whose branches droop heavy-laden with the abundant fruit of naked cupids. (*Rien n'habille comme le nu,* says Voltaire.) The inner quadrangle opens into Old World classrooms, cloister-like in primitive simplicity, their only furnishing uneasy ax-hewn wooden benches, possibly befitting a university largely endowed during the ascetic rule of the Catholic kings. There is something pitifully sad about this vast monastic building, quiet and deserted save for an occasional group of students in cap and gown on their silent way to a gloomy, sparsely filled classroom. It is as difficult to realize that this was once the center of the world's learning, as that the statue of Fray Louis de León, Sala-

303

manca's favorite son and Spain's great lyric
poet, which stands in front of the university, was
erected in memory of his long imprisonment by
the Inquisition for having dared to translate
the Songs of Solomon. O shade of Anthony
Comstock!

There is an old song that sings of Salamanca's
falling asleep to the sound of the guitar and
awakening to the voices of students; but serenades from black-gowned *estudiantes* are rarely
heard nowadays. Strangely enough, however,
we were aroused every morning by a slow,
monotonous chant of voices from a school across
the way, where the master, after reading out a
lesson, made the pupils recite it aloud. For
hours the school window sent forth a wearisome
singsong of constant repetition. Without moving, the poor youngsters kept on repeating the
same tiresome words, the running chorus only
now and then stilled by some criticism or correc-
tion from the instructor—a system introduced
by the Moors centuries ago, one book serving
for all.

It is scarcely worthy of a great nation such as
Spain that education in many Spanish provinces
is still decidedly backward. This is partly due
to the old-time beggarly, long-unpaid salaries.

"Tiene más hambre que un maestro de escuela"
(He is hungrier than a schoolmaster), is a popular saying. Even now, after years of reform and
a lavish increase in remuneration, only one hundred and sixty dollars yearly is paid a beginner.
Though primary education is obligatory by law,
the application of the law is purely theoretical,
for the reason that many villages have not sufficient official funds to afford even these miserable
salaries. And not only are school buildings
scandalously insufficient, but more often than
not they are at impossible distances from the
scattered pupils. Also, through ignorance or
from dire necessity, especially in the farming
country where children are obliged to help,
many of the girls and boys are put to work as
soon as they are physically able, with the result,
according to the *Anuario Estadistico de España,*
issued in April, 1922, that out of a total population of 19,995,686 there were 11,867,455 unable
either to read or write.

Statistics, however, have a dishonest way of
telling half truths, and the *Anuario* gives not the
vaguest hint of the marvelous progress made in
Catalonia. Weary of waiting for the Central
Government to take action, the province, with
patriotic devotion, has locally taxed itself, rais-

ing funds for model institutions of which the influence is being felt throughout the entire country. In Catalonia, the problem of education has taken firm root, shooting forth branches in every direction, not alone along the road of primary instruction, but on the higher routes of technical and scientific teaching, and with schools of art that have brought to light the mines of artistic wealth with which Catalonia is endowed. There are schools for women, which are inspiring a new way of living, consigning to the past the old rigid paths of the dark ages, along which, until fairly recent years, Spanish women were expected to plod through life.

A cheery-faced, tattered little lad of eleven awaits outside the hotel entrance, plaintively eager to guide the strangers on their ramble among the eternal beauties of lovely, timeworn Salamanca. As the oldest of ten he must help support the family, even though his father, so he proudly tells us, earns two and one half pesetas a day (worth fifty cents in normal times). What is his name? Jesús María, chosen by a religious mother before he was born as appropriate to either boy or girl. Who said the Spaniards lacked a sense of humor?

Actual hunger showed on that proud little face, but it took long questioning before he would acknowledge that he had had no breakfast. So it was that we went at once to the fine old Plaza Mayor, where, under pillared colonnades, was found a café supplying "mouthfuls," as the Spanish call sandwiches—huge rolls, stuffed thick with meat, a decidedly big mouthful for our little lad. Between happy bites, and pointing out with his disengaged hand a small house plastered with a coat of arms that looked like raised embroidery, he managed to mumble inarticulately the story of its one-time owner.

Doña María la Brava, a widow, had two sons, both of whom belonged to the ruling Blancas, one of the two warlike cliques which at that time guided the destinies of Salamanca. As boys, these sons of Doña María had become friendly with two brothers belonging to the rival group,—the Rojas,—who, later in life, when a fierce quarrel arose between the two enemy factions, proved that, before anything else, they were worthy supporters of their party's strifes, not hesitating to kill their old-time friends. Even though there was no man left in the enemy family to avenge the outrage, the Roja brothers fled to Portugal for safety.

307

When the dead bodies of her two sons were laid at Doña María's feet, not a tear showed upon the stern old face. Calmly she told the bearers to carry her sons to the cathedral, while she gathered together an armed force, declaring that from that time she lived only for vengeance. When her retainers told her that the murderers were by then safe in Portugal, she answered that nothing in this world was so strong as a mother's heart, and what that heart earnestly desires, it will get. "I will dress as a man, act as your leader, and in all times of danger be at the front." And so she did, proceeding by forced march to Portugal, where, discovering the hiding place of her son's slayers, she managed to force an entrance.

The two young men were taken by surprise, and after a brief struggle, Doña María hung their bloody severed heads at her girdle. Returning to Salamanca, she at once went to the cathedral and placed the gory trophy upon her sons' tombs, and then—and not till then, says the chronicle—she gave way to tears.

Even today a *charro,* as he passes on his way home from market, may be heard to sing a verse of that poem legend written over three centuries ago:

No llora la gran matrona
Al ver sus pechos abiertos;
Que, en no llorar hijos muertos
Quiere ser más que leona.

"You are Americans, are you not?" asks our little guide, very distinctly, now that the second "mouthful" has disappeared. And, without waiting, as though certain of the answer, he pilots the way to the Dominican Convent of San Estéban, decorated with golden figures of heraldic monsters. Jesús María has to stand on tiptoe to ring the entrance bell, and when a rotund, white-robed padre opens the door, he gleefully shouts the news that we come from *Los Estados Unidos.* In silence we pass through the cloisters where Christopher Columbus walked in consultation with the great Dominican de Doza, after this erudite friar had given the "Dreamer" his friendship and support; then into the long council room to which, by order of King Ferdinand, Columbus was brought before a great gathering of learned men and ecclesiastics, in a vain attempt to win their favor for his splendid vision.

"There is but one world," contemptuously replied Salamanca's savants, who considered Columbus presumptuous and visionary.

"There are two," doggedly insisted the

Dreamer, and, to the confusion of these wise men, there were two.

After viewing the famous Casa de las Conchas, a house thickly sprinkled with shells of stone so delicately wrought that the sunlight filters through them,—the dream house of a pilgrim, for shells, you remember, are the emblem of pilgrimages,—we wander in the two cathedrals, the new and the old, the very new dating from 1500. But it is the old which holds us the longer; its massive walls a golden glow warmed by the sun of nearly nine hundred years. Within is a "decorated delirium" of fabulous men and beasts chasing one another from pillar to pillar, a fantastic display seldom seen outside of Spain.

Only at nightfall do we turn back to the plaza, now gay with evening loiterers. Looking through the broad entrance arch brightly illuminated by electric light, it seems like the stage of some great theater upon which the curtain has just risen—the very picture one strives to carry away in his book of memories.

June 1

As the crow flies—the road as straight as though traced with a cord—we roll through fields and fields of light green dotted with poppies like spots of blood. A country of dreamy sadness, where the soul of the traveler drowses. There are few people; only now and then a man or woman, riding donkeys, pass and salute with gravity. The far-apart villages sleep so profoundly that one can scarcely hear the breathing of the sleepers. Only at Tordesillas are men and women spying out at us from high breathing holes that serve as windows. Here children turn out, offering to show the town where Juana the Mad lived. They point to the not distant Castillo de la Mata, where the great Queen Isabella, Juana's mother, died—alone except for servants. Her only son and her best beloved daughter were both dead; Juana, her only remaining child, was mad; and Ferdinand, her husband, far away, fighting the enemies of his country, was as well resisting the budding passion for eighteen-year-old Germaine of France —whom he later married with such indecent haste. How pitiful a finis to so glorious a life book!

We are now in Valladolid, the city of that famous company who played the leading rôles in the great dramas of the fifteenth and sixteenth centuries.

311

Here Columbus died, Philip the Second was born, and Cervantes published *Don Quixote*. Here was laid the scene of the epic meeting of Isabella and Ferdinand, as well as the romantic tragedy of Blanche of Navarre; Lesage made Valladolid the city where Gil Blas, one of the great characters in fiction, practiced physics under the withered Doctor Sangrado, the forerunner of the undertaker, whose remedy for obstructed perspiration was to drink water by the pailful. Here lived the great dramatist, Calderon; the splendid painter, Alonzo Cano; the famous Cardinal Ziminez; and the infamous fanatic Torquemada, who created the Tribunal of Inquisition, condemning the city to live for all time among the spirits of slaughtered men and making it impossible for the superstitious to sleep by night because of the awful groans of the tortured.

Valladolid was long the center of the dreaded *Auto da Fé* (Act of Faith), which sought to save souls by destroying bodies. Let us wander back in thought to that fête day in the year 1599, when the great Plaza Mayor was being made ready for its sacrifice by fire. Two vast stages built face to face are already in place. One is for penitents—those admitted to public penance in hopes of a change in heart. Escorted by Dominican attendants, the "watchdogs of God," they totter with faltering steps to the supporting rail that surrounds the platform. In front of the other stage—for Inquisitors and secular authorities—there stands a sort of pulpit covered with black cloth, holding the box of condemnation—a crimson velvet casket fringed with gold, out of which, one by one, the dread decrees will be taken and read aloud by a ghastly figure swathed in burial clothes.

At the extreme right there has been staked off a small enclosure in which are piles of fagots heaped high against iron posts securely fastened to the ground; and as though fearful of lacking fuel, several troops of asses laden with extra firewood are tethered close at hand, serenely munching, in happy oblivion of the tragedy to come. On guard about the enclosure is a company of soldiers armed with matchlock harquebuses. It is a setting worthy of the terrors on the last Day of Judgment.

Every window in the plaza is filled, until the very walls seem clothed with the morbid faces of spectators. Even the roofs of the houses are black with onlookers, for the clergy, by threats, oblige the people to attend. King Philip is there, of course, as well as the Grandees of Spain, and all the court. The clergy too, brilliant in sacerdotal robes, are prepared to take part in the pompous ceremonial which the Church of Rome can so well display on fitting occasions.

To the mournful tolling of bells, a gruesome procession headed by all the city's crosses, shrouded in black, slowly approaches. First are those penitents who are to be "reconciled"— restored to the Church. Some are bared to the waist, astride asses; about their necks are halters with one, two, and three knots in the rope, each knot indicating two hundred lashes—a sentence carried out, as the procession proceeds, by executioners with steel-knobbed leather straps. Only by the help of "Pie de Amigos"—iron instruments held by guards riding alongside— can these nearly unconscious men be kept erect. Others, who are "reconciled" with less severity, wear cone-shaped miters inscribed with their names in letters of red. Town criers march beside the penitents, proclaiming their offenses.

Last come the penitents who are to be "relaxed"—handed over to the civil authorities to expiate their religious crimes. One by one, each escorted by two friars carrying the standards of

the Inquisition, they march to their doom, forced
to bear green crosses, emblems of the most
poisonous blasphemy, to render them as odious
as possible to the superstitious crowd. They
are made more repulsive by the only covering
for their nakedness—a single sack-like garment
of coarse yellow weave, on which is embroidered a group of grinning red devils playing
with flames of fire, a presage of their future.

On arriving in the plaza, and taking their
prescribed places, the sentences are publicly
read. Then a few of the "relaxed" are mercifully strangled, but the remainder are cast into
the soldier-guarded square, where their impious
bodies are reduced to ashes and later scattered in
oblivion over the fields beyond.

But everything in life has its reverse side, and
so wherever shadows are deepest, there is certain to be found light. As we stand in front of
the Royal Palace, we see quite another picture,
the romantic courtship and betrothal of Ferdinand and Isabella, which *Old Court Life in
Spain* graphically paints, finding the colors in
the pigment box of ancient chronicles.

The Convent of San Pablo, immediately
opposite the palace, whose midnight bells

sounded the hour for the meeting of Ferdinand
and Isabella, has a decidedly self-conscious air,
mindful that it possesses one of the most fantastic church faces the world has ever seen—a
"tortured" collection of figures, against a background of delicate stone embroidery, tinged by
age to a silver tone—a most superb example of
Spain's famous *platearesque* (silversmith) style.

A step or two beyond, and the Colegio de San
Gregorio rises in defiant rivalry to San Pablo's
wealth of ornamentation; its façade positively
glutted by extravagant carving. Heraldic
shields, armorial bearings, and bizarre crests
emblazon the stone wall in an arrogant enthusiasm for religion,—the "pride of humility." This
was characteristic of Philip the Second, who
first saw the light of day as it filtered through
the quaint angle windows of the low-roofed
house on the plaza corner, an oriel of such exquisite charm as to suit better some beautiful
queen than so dismal a king. Philip's only passion was a perverted religion, his enthusiasm
leading him not only to burn the followers of
Mahomet, but even to destroy their bathtubs, as
though anything indulged in by heretics must
needs be ungodly. It was in this fashion it came
about that medieval Christianity looked upon

bathing as an irreligious custom, one sainted lady proudly recording the fact that during her entire life of seventy years she never washed more than the tips of two fingers, and that, in preparation for receiving mass. The sanctity of her followers was to be measured by how closely they dared to approach! This dogma of fanaticism fixed its roots so firmly in the soil of Spanish life that even to this day bathing facilities are comparatively limited, and when provided, they are hesitatingly used by conservative Spaniards as flying directly in the face of Providence.

Due to this same unsympathetic spirit, Valladolid permitted Columbus to die in obscurity and neglect. On his return from the fourth voyage, Isabella was no longer his constant friend and protector; he received nothing from Ferdinand but empty words; and the man who had brought untold wealth to Spain had to live, broken-hearted, on borrowed money, realizing in the disillusioning realities of life how little gratitude exists in the world. Even the house in which he lived is almost forgotten.

In strange contrast with this is the Casa de Cervantes, where lived Spain's other immortal son. His house is carefully preserved and splendidly restored, possibly because Cervantes

317

showed in his books a lasting affection for Valladolid, in whose streets he ran about as a boy, and where, as a man, after the opening chapters of his great work had been published, he received the first fruits of an imperishable glory.

Though the average Spaniard goes to the theater to be amused rather than instructed, the plays of Cervantes still hold the stage of Valladolid's famous old Teatro de Calderón, one of the largest in Spain. Evening performances seldom begin before ten o'clock—rather early for the ordinary Spaniard, who never dines until nine, more frequently at ten. This habit of late dining has made popular the custom of going to the theater by the hour—to little playlets, or *zarzuelas* (operettas), lasting just that length of time. They allow one to stroll in at the hour most convenient, to stay for one play, and then to visit with some friend at the club, returning, perhaps, for another play after eleven, when the themes chosen are more in accordance with the taste of the man about town. The last play is invariably followed by a long séance at some café,—always crowded until the "small hours," —with most of the frequenters, in riotous dissipation, drinking cup after cup of chocolate

318

while they excitedly discuss every known topic from the fall of the Ministry to the immaculate conception.

An early summer morning, a sky pure, without stain, and the silence and solitude of Old Castile. Golden seas of wheat stretch into the far distance until lost in the blue horizon. Grain, nothing but grain in this Tierra de Campos, glistening with living flame as the sunned breeze strikes it. Hardly a tree in all the wide expanse. Speak of trees to the peasants and they will make a sign of the cross, saying if they plant trees, birds will come, and if birds come, Castile will be lost. But there are few peasants to whom to speak; the men and women who labor here live in towns far apart, and after the harvest those fields will be entirely without movement—desolate and forgotten, like some useless mirror cracked by the sun.

The faces of the rare passers-by are singularly grave and serious, an inheritance of this austere province from which sprang the only real resistance against enemy invasion—from here went forth those who, with lance in hand, retook from the Moors kingdom after kingdom.

319

Those who love the poetry of medieval days should visit these romantic plains where legend is preserved in all primeval pureness. They overflow with historic marvels and jewels of sentimental value, scarcely known by name except to the peasants in these little hamlets. At Villasurgas they will point out the beautiful Romanic porch of Santa María, which tells in words of stone the story of the four maidens of Carrión, that little village's share of the hundred Christian Virgins demanded in yearly tribute by the Moor conquerors—long time a law in the land. As the Nubian eunuchs, gathering together the cursed tribute, were passing through these plains of Carrión, wild bulls, guided by the hand of Him who orders the life of all, fiercely attacked the Moorish collectors, scattering them in flight. They then stood on guard beside the maidens until help came and they were carried into the village, where a church was built in memory of this miraculous happening. On the cornice of the porch decorated with the figures of these Christian martyrs may be seen the heads of wild bulls, still watchfully on guard.

For miles we wind between fields of wheat, green and level as the top of a billiard table;

and then we espy a cross which signals the entrance to Las Huelgas, so poetical from afar, but, like so much else in the world, converted into prose on near approach. These one-time gay, Old World pleasure grounds (Las Huelgas) with a château for the delight of kings, is now a silent place, the most famous nunnery in Spain, surrounded by high walls like some prison. In olden time within its convent chapel, esquires, on the eve of knighthood, kept vigil through the night, their armor placed on the resplendent altar, before which they would kneel, vowing to live a life of chastity and to serve mankind. Just at dawn they would reverently approach the image of Saint James, the warrior saint, whose arms, moved by secret springs, caused the sword fastened to his right hand to fall gently upon the shoulder of the youthful aspirant, conferring upon him the honor of knighthood.

The Capilla Mayor, into which no man may enter save the king, is barricaded by a heavy grating hung with violet draperies brilliantly woven with threads of color. Peering between the curtains, we see amid a blaze of golden sunset the gentle-born sisters, for none but noble ladies belong to this exclusive cloister, as, silently, they file into their ancient stalls for vespers. Beautiful voices flood the building, soaring heavenward in an attempt to voice the inexpressible, so quickening the imagination that, as Azorin says, we seem to be listening to the soul of things, to feel yearnings never before known, to desire something we cannot define. Does not this explain, mayhap, that fugitive craving for life that now and again seems to color those blanched faces? But the cloister walls are heavy, the moment passes, and the placid sisters continue to dream—until when?

Proceeding along the way, we too dream, for the mere sight of Burgos, in the distance, inevitably evokes memories of the Cid, the strands of whose romantic life are so closely interwoven with the historic threads of the city as to make it fairly impossible to disentangle one from the other. At Burgos the Cid was born, at Burgos he was married, and in the great cathedral of Burgos he has found his final resting place.

According to the ancient chronicle, Rodrigo Diaz de Vivar was a mere youth when he challenged and killed the great Count Gomez, who had grievously insulted his father, too old to

AIRPLANE VIEW OF BURGOS, THE CATHEDRAL IN THE CENTER.

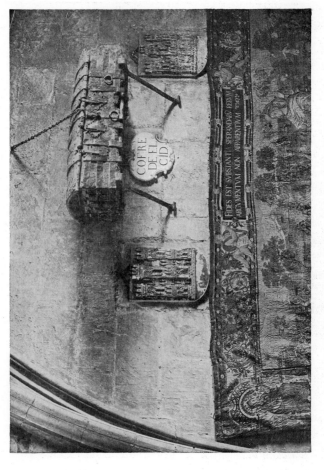

COFFER OF EL CID IN BURGOS CATHEDRAL

fight on his own behalf. Beautiful Ximena, the Count's daughter, boldly confronted him in the public square, defiantly bidding him to kill her as he had killed her father. "Don't spare me because I am a woman," she exclaimed. His youthful ardor was kindled, and it was love, not anger, that filled his heart. Fearing to betray himself, he answered nothing. Whereupon Ximena some time later went to the King and demanded justice. The King was sore perplexed, knowing that if he punished Rodrigo, the people would revolt, for already his fame had spread over the land. But as he anxiously pondered upon what answer to give, the feelings of Ximena underwent a remarkable change. Contritely she fell upon her knees before the King, craving a boon. "O Sire," she implored, "give to me as husband the man who killed my father, for I begin to believe that he who has brought so much sorrow has the power to bring much happiness." The poor King, says the chronicle, was completely overcome, so extraordinary is the inconsistency of woman, one moment asking for a man's life, another demanding his hand in marriage.

Now at this time Rodrigo was away fighting the Moors, gaining in acknowledgment of his prowess the Arabic title of *Sid (Cid)*, "Lord and Conqueror." Later he added the surname *El Campeador,* "Champion," being always the first to offer to fight in single contest before a general engagement. This was the custom in his day, just as, centuries before, Goliath had stood before the hosts of Israel.

On his return from the wars the king summoned Rodrigo to appear at court, and he was greatly relieved to find the Cid right willing to take Ximena for wife. When, by the king's order, the two were brought face to face, the Cid spake first. "Fair lady, I slew a man; I owe a man, and, by God's grace, an honored husband thou shalt have in thy dear father's place."

The wedding was celebrated with great magnificence, the streets were hung with tapestry and velvets, all the bells of the city were rung, and every house was brilliantly illuminated. In the language of the "Romancero del Cid," one of the oldest poems in the Spanish tongue:

The King had taken order that they should rear an arch
From house to house all over in the way where they must
 march
They have hung it all with lances and shields and glittering
 helms
Brought by the Campeador from out Moorish realms.

324

They have scattered olive branches and rushes on the street
And the ladies fling down garlands at the Campeador's feet
With tapestry and broidery their balconies between
To do his bridal honour their walls the Burghers screen.

Some years after, when Don Sancho, the patron of the Cid and the brother of King Alfonso, was foully murdered in Zamora, the King was suspected of having a hand in his death. The Cid refused to do him homage or kiss his hand until he cleared himself by oath in the Church of San Gadea—still standing on the hill above the cathedral. The accusation being so very grave, the King was not allowed to take the oath of purgation alone, but had to be supported by twelve of his knights, the greatest and most powerful in the kingdom. They must swear with him as to the truth of his oath, and, in the Middle Ages, the administration of oaths was surrounded by such awe and solemnity that no one would dare to swear falsely lest the vengeance of God overtake them.

All the people had been summoned to be present at the ceremony, and at the church a goodly company were awaiting, when the twelve knights approached slowly on horseback, each horse being led by a brightly appareled page. They were followed by two foot soldiers, one bearing their master's shield, lavishly adorned with gold and silver, the other, his tournament spear set with streamers. Prominent among these Hidalgos might be seen the flashing eye and tall stature of El Cid, sheathed in golden mail bright as the sun, over which hung an ermine cloak.

Communion was administered, and then the King strode to the high staging erected in the center of the church, so that all could see him. The Cid followed, standing directly in front, holding a crucifix and a book of the Gospels, upon which the King placed his hand. As he took the solemn oath, the Cid cried aloud: "If thou speakest not the truth, may the Knaves of Asturia tear out thy heart and may you die unshriven." The Cid made him repeat the oath a second and even a third time, until the wrath of the King was so exceeding great that then and there he banished the Cid from his kingdom. So unexpectedly did this command come that the Cid found himself without the necessary money. But luckily he bethought him of a plan for procuring it.

Taking a great chest of gold and red leather, nail-fastened and tipped with bands of iron, he filled it to the brim with sand and rocks, tightly locking it. Then he summoned two rich Jews, Rachael and Vidas, telling them he could not carry his treasures with him into exile, but if they would lend him a thousand pieces of gold they might keep the jewels and plate as security. The Jews, trying to raise the chest, found it so heavy as to require six horses to carry it away, and they gleefully gave him the money he asked, being full glad of the bargain. Be it known that today, within the cathedral, fastened to the wall of the Capilla del Corpus Cristi, is this coffer of the Cid, accepted by the Church as authentic.

Then came many years of fighting, victory always following the banner of the Cid until at the height of glory, as Conqueror of Valencia, a greater conquistador, Death, overcame him. All Spain mourned his demise. His body was carried to the convent church of San Pedro de Cardena. Here, clothed in a fine suit of armor, with his double-hilted sword, Tizona, clutched in one hand, in appearance the same as on leaving Valencia, he was seated on his ivory chair of state in the center of the nave—his body being so carefully embalmed that it showed no signs of dissolution. One day, says the chronicle, a Jew entered this sanctuary to look upon the dead hero's body. When he saw the mighty warrior sitting there with the same old arrogant expression on his face, anger stirred his heart, and he cried aloud: "So thou art the great Cid who forced my brethren to lend you good golden pieces upon false pretenses. You proudly asserted that the hand of Moor or Jew never dared to touch that once thick black beard of thine. Now thy beard is thin and gray, and thou art at my feet, and the hand of a Jew dares to touch it." A gurgling sound was heard, the Jew fell to the ground in a fit, and one of the attendant priests rushing in at the sound saw that the dead hand had drawn the sword a good foot from the scabbard.

For many years the body of the Cid—and that of Ximena, his wife—rested in the Church of San Pedro; but last summer, on the seven hundredth anniversary of the foundation of the lovely cathedral of Burgos, the scattered remains of the Cid were buried in its crypt, with all fitting ceremony.

Certainly no more worthy resting place for Spain's warrior-idol could possibly be found. Burgos is supreme among Spanish Gothic cathedrals and one of the most perfect in Europe, although, as usual, mean buildings are crowded around it as if in humble kneeling adoration.

BURGOS CATHEDRAL

PINNACLES OF ONE OF THE TOWERS OF BURGOS CATHEDRAL,
EACH SPIRE SURMOUNTED BY A STATUE.

Spain repeats to this day the old Castilian saying, "It makes little difference if my home be small and poor, provided the house of God is rich," and Burgos assuredly has carried precept into practice. Two delicate-pointed spires of stone lace-work pierce the sky, overtopping a forest of other pinnacles, all faceted like precious stones and chiseled as daintily as a woman's bracelet or some chased reliquary. Through the open-work embroidery of the soft-hued steeples, the angel blue of the sky peeps down at us as with the eyes of heaven. A fairy building all "lace and light" without, while within, where usually is found the subdued atmosphere of mystery such as the Spaniard believes alone befits an attitude of prayer, there is a sweet benediction of light revealing all the intricate and restless splendor of this glorious temple. Even at sundown, beneath the lantern that Philip the Second in one of his rarely happy moods likened to the work of angels, the light clings on long after the aisles are in shadow.

Did the master builders think they had nothing to do but carve statues? Every high ledge and inaccessible corner has its image. It is as if all the saints, prophets, and seraphs in Christendom had been winging about the sacred enclos-

329

ure and had just alighted for a moment's rest.
Within the chapels among their lavish display
of regal tombs, where princes, bishops, and
kings sleep their everlasting sleep, there is a
profusion of carven effigies that gaze out with
mystic expression, striving to reveal the hidden
secrets of eternity.

But the imagination at length grows weary
in breathless admiration. We turn away, going to the gay promenade between whispering
poplars, where all of Burgos loiters, even though
this June day finds them *embozados en la capa*
(muffled up in heavy cloaks), their very mouths
wrapped about as though the delightful mountain air came from some plague-stricken lowland. It is claimed that the sun, like everything
else, has to be imported into Burgos, whose
climate, according to the popular phrase, is,
Nueve meses de invierno, tres de infierno (Nine
of winter and three of hell).

June 15

Retracing our road until it swings northward
toward Palencia, we reach a great plain of blazing poppies. According to Spanish folklore,
they grow in such luxuriance only where much
blood has been spilled. It was in these flaming

fields that Mad Juana spent the night rather than shelter in a convent of nuns the faithless body of her husband, that she was bringing from Burgos.

On the way she stopped at Miraflores, the summit of a chalky wind-swept hill, where had been built a monastery of gray stone, harsh and stern to the eye, but peopled by simple-hearted Carthusians, who filled it with the peace of great sacrifice. It shelters magnificent tombs, sumptuous and richly wrought, erected by the order of the great Isabella as monuments to her parents. They claim to be the finest and most elaborate sculpture of their kind in the world. How great in contrast is the little mud-walled cemetery where, amid a tangle of weeds, humble and forgotten, lie hundreds of Carthusian monks! There you find no pompous language of epitaph, neither name nor date, nothing to recall death, only an agreeable sadness, a melancholy quiet, unbroken save for the occasional peck-peck of a bird as it snaps at an insect on the moss-covered walls, and the sunning lizards scurry in fright to their refuge cracks.

Philip, the handsomest man in Europe, was a worthless profligate, and Juana, his wife, who responded to his unfaithfulness with a blind, pas-

sionate devotion, went mad from jealousy.
When Philip died, Juana was like a raging
lioness deprived of its whelp. She insisted upon
being constantly with her husband, never permitting herself to be separated from his body
which, wonderfully embalmed, lay in a glass-
lidded coffin, covered with the green and red
gold-embroidered curtains of their marriage'
couch. And when Juana happened to overhear
the discussion of a plan for taking Philip to
Flanders, his one-time home, she hurriedly
caused the coffin to be placed on a bier platform
and carried it away, accompanied by his erst-
while pages and suite.

As if he were alive, they stopped at the
Cartuja de Miraflores, whose venerable prior,
white-robed and white-bearded, in a pious effort to bring comfort, had the unfortunate
thought of suggesting that the dead body of
Philip might be resuscitated. That hope became a fixed idea in the poor mad brain of Juana,
and at every stop thereafter she opened the coffin
to see if her husband had come to life. The
lamentable cortège traveled only by night, for,
said Juana, a woman who has lost her husband,
the sun of her life, should not see the light of
day. Always jealous, she would not allow a

woman even to approach her husband's coffin.
Once when they had halted for rest at a convent,
upon finding it was a convent of nuns, Juana
immediately left, though the night was cold and
stormy.

Pradilla's famous picture in the Prado at
Madrid depicts Juana in these poppy fields near
Palencia just after she had fled from the convent. The sky is somber with lowering, sullen
clouds. Deep ruts show in the rain-soaked
ground. Around little fires of wet, smoldering
fagots, the weary attendants are crouching.
In the foreground, on a white, silk-covered
stretcher, is the coffin, decorated with the golden
eagle of Austria and the lion of Aragon. At
each of the four corners are iron candelabra
with candles that flicker and gutter in the rush
of the night air, as if about to expire. Mad
Juana, dressed in black velvet, about her head
a wind-flying veil, stands close to the bier; sor-
rowed by the evening storm, she gazes incon-
solably into the night. A scene of immense
desolation.

And hardly less dreary is the "ague-feeding
lake of Nava," serving as a mirror for the
rickety shacks lining its banks, shacks from out

of which rush dogs that run after us at full cry. Curious, how here in the North the dogs always jump up and bark and run; while in Castile, though they jump up and bark, they never run. In Toledo they may move their heads, but they do not get up; and as for Andalusia, there they open but one eye, only to close it again and fall asleep.

Equally dreary are the dilapidated ruins of the Benedictine Abbey of Sahagun, once first in wealth and dignity in all of Spain. Dreary also the low, flat, partly inundated land, looking as if nature had grown tired and didn't care.

"But how poor are they who have not patience!" In good time pleasant fields bordered by long lines of high poplars show in the distance, and the road leads to León.

12

Asturias and Journey's End

Azorin, Spain's master essayist, whose pure, beautiful style has carried him into the ranks of the illustrious literati, writes of León as a city cold and deserted, whose streets have ceased to live centuries ago. Perhaps from time to time, he says, a great portal turns on its rusty hinges and a silent old woman appears in the monumental doorway, or some gaudy government building breaks the harmony and sends a breeze of modern frivolity through the old stones. No one crosses the square, its life has passed away. The towers, the little roofs, the grated windows and protruding balconies remain in an atmosphere that is not theirs.

But cities, like individuals, have faces that each one reads differently, and León gives us a warm and noisy welcome. From all sides come cries of "¡Sale mañana! ¿Quien quiere la suerte?"—"A drawing tomorrow, who wants the lucky number?" And before we have time to leave the automobile, one of life's wrecks, in tattered rags of a tint that could come only from long exposure, her sunken bloodshot eyes lighted with the fire of avarice, clutches my sleeve and hoarsely whispers, *"Tengo el gordo"* (It is I who hold the fat prize).

Three times a month the national lottery has a drawing, and although tickets are thrust under one's nose any day and all day, it is the day before the drawing that every city, town, and village seethes with excitement—the gambling spirit has bitten deep into the very heart of Spain. However, it is only fair to state that the lottery is conducted with absolute honesty, and it is also safeguarded by every possible precaution.

Once at Madrid, in the Casa de la Moneda, where the *sorteo* or official drawings take place, we watched this classic ceremony surrounded by all the pomp and form Spain loves so well. The little room was packed, with an overflow into the hall, and even half filling the great square beyond. On a raised platform, behind a long table sat the Board of Administration, solemnly watching the proceedings. White pierced balls stamped with black figures duplicating the numbered tickets sold broadcast throughout the country had been strung on wires hanging from a locked frame, immediately above a huge tub. At a signal from the President of the Board the frame is unlocked, and the numbered balls drop into the mixing trough with a deafening rattle. Men with wooden spades turn them over and over until they are well mingled. Then from a huge wire sphere of fine open mesh a carrier drops into the tub and sucks it empty. The globe, locked, begins to revolve rapidly, further mixing the numbers. From this, by enclosed carrier, a smaller globe, also suspended from the ceiling, is filled full. These are the winning numbers. This ceremony finished, the hundreds of prizes to each *sorteo,* marked on the same-sized white balls that carry the ticket numbers, are dropped one by one into the now empty tub, the amount of each prize being read aloud as it falls. Then these too are shot into the big globe, which is again furiously shaken.

The stage is now set for the dramatic climax. Four children from the State Orphan Asylum are led into the room; one is stationed at each globe, two are at a table between. The boy at the big globe touches a spring at the bottom, permitting one ball to fall. A ball drops. Clutched tightly in his little hand, he passes it to his comrades at the table, who read the marking. One by one the balls are withdrawn, until a prize appears, when the boy at the small globe presses his spring and the number which is to win that particular prize comes forth. For hours this tense excitement reigns. Nothing is heard but the monotonous, tremulous voices of the boys. Their task, by the way, is eagerly sought after, for they may safely rely upon the life patronage of any big winner, and the first prize of the Christmas lottery is big—15,000,000 pesetas.

This lottery was created back in 1763, with the idea of contributing to the upkeep of charitable institutions, and although it undoubtedly foments the gambling spirit rife in Spain without encouragement, the people look upon it as a sort of tax disguised in pleasurable coating. If statistics are to be believed, it has not prejudiced the principle of saving, and last year the Government received in revenue 222,000,000 pesetas.

If it be true that after uniting the Crowns of León and Castile, Ferdinand the Third, in abandoning the ancient seat of the monarchy felt compassion—as a generous sovereign should —for a beloved servitor forced into retirement

CATHEDRAL OF LEÓN

MONASTERY AT OVIEDO

and pensioned León with her cathedral, he built so that even today the city, standing apart, withered with the chill of old age, remains everlastingly unforgetable. Faith was gloriously generous when she offered to Our Lady of the Blanca this masterpiece of "frozen music," likened in its aërial daintiness to the frost pattern on a windowpane. But if her beauty rests on daring lightness, certainly her glory lies within the resplendent stained glass that of a late afternoon shivers the light into a thousand iridescent bits, painting the walls and pavement with jeweled color. Just the mise-en-scène for the bishop, gorgeous in crimson silk, with scarlet-clothed acolytes carrying the long train of his red robe, as he is conducted in state from his throne beside the altar to his palace over the courtyard. Here gayly robed peasants throng about to kiss the episcopal ring.

But if you seek the ancient spirit of old León, you must look for it behind the darkly tinged monastery of San Isidro, whose walls are covered with curious stiff Byzantine frescoes, a place so holy that it enjoys the rare privilege of having the host perpetually *de manifesto*. You will be told the awesome story of how on the eve of the momentous battle of Las Navas de

Tolosa the clang of armor and the tramp of horses and men were heard throughout the slumbering city; that a phantom army stopped at the monastery gate, beat a thundering summons at the door, and called upon the priest who was keeping vigil, saying that they had come for King Fernando, who lay buried within, to rise and ride with them to the help of Spain in her sore need. The terrified monk fell fainting to the ground. When he revived, the tomb stood open—the last ghostly recruit had joined the colors. The following morning his spirit appeared in the heavens encouraging the Christian soldiers and leading them to victory. Even so it was in the World War, that the spirit of Christ was said to have hovered over a handful of despairing Englishmen fighting against great odds.

June 17

Soon after leaving León, the ground became like a troubled ocean, every earthy wave bearing us higher and higher, until the rugged arms of mountains held us in stony embrace, wrapping us about with a perfect labyrinth of Alpine heights, where the keen, biting air, the music of falling water, and the sweep of a sea wind gladdens the senses long dimmed by the sad desolation of Castile.

This magnificent route over the Cantabrian range is called *Camino de Plata* (Street of Silver), so great was the cost. It is always winding up and down, through narrow, rocky gorges, over romantic bridges, coiling serpentlike round otherwise inaccessible rock masses crowned by eternal snow. In scenic charm the road is probably the most beautiful in Spain, if not in Europe, rivaling Switzerland and her mountain slopes, and out-rivaling her with a near-by sea that batters against the lower foothills.

In such homes of solitude we meet more than the usual number of those black, white, and yellow uniformed *Guardia Civil* who are spread over all the land on constant watch. A small army of veteran soldiers they are, splendidly mounted, magnificently trained, living under the strictest military regulations. Their first article of faith insists upon the maintenance of honor at any cost, with complete self-sacrifice when demanded by duty or danger. They have been granted the power of life and death, each carrying a gun that he knows how to use, and when they shoot, no explanation is asked. To

341

the customary word of leave-taking, *Hasta mañana!* (Until tomorrow), the usual peasant addition is, "If it be the will of God—and the *Guardia Civil!*"

The need for these guardians is shown by the all too frequent thin mounds of earth, six feet by one, alongside the road, marked with a tiny slab bearing the words *aquí muerto.* These tell the story of some wayside murder—it being the custom in these parts to bury a man on the spot where he met his death.

But whosoever lies there has the best of it. For him, no clammy sepulcher among other hideous graves marked with falsities, but just a rough stone, the wide sky, and nature's blessing.

These mountains are the cradle of the Spanish nation, the birthplace of the oldest blood in the country—idyllic Asturias. Since the fourteenth century it has given its name to the heir apparent. At that time a daughter of an English duke was about to be married to one of Spain's kings. Her father insisted upon a clause in the marriage settlements that would grant to the prospective son a title equal to that of "Prince of Wales." And so it is that the present son of another Englishwoman,—Victoria,—the daughter of another English duke, is known as "Prince of Asturias."

In Oviedo, the capital of the province, modern industry, called progress, is fast sweeping away all traces of the picturesque past. If, by chance, you happen to stumble upon an old, crooked street, it immediately leads into a straight new boulevard, showy with glittering plate glass. The blame is laid upon the "Americans," as they call those who, early in life, emigrated, made good, and in their old age returned home to flaunt their good fortune in the faces of less adventurous neighbors.

These soldiers of fortune imbued with modernism preach "change" at all times and in all places, but many of the stay-at-homes are unchangeable so far as customs go. Last night from a balcony above our hotel window came the disturbing sound of a lurid love-making. Across the square on another balcony stands the fair one. The two, unabashedly, shoot tender messages back and forth. When they have emptied their batteries of love, there is a silence, but only just long enough to recharge, and the firing begins again. We look out, to see a watching Serano, quaint in antique cloak and broad-brimmed hat, slouching across the plaza,

giving the reassuring cry of "All Serene!" For
the lovers, yes; but for us! The love serenade
sounded in our sleepless ears until almost
morning.

Untouched also by modern skepticism is the
Camara Santa in the cathedral, filled with the
"marvels of God"—the holiest relics in Spain.
After the sack of Jerusalem, all these miracle-
working wonders found a home in the churches
of the South, being brought into Asturias by the
faithful when they fled before the invading
Moors. Since that time they have been safeguarded by Oviedo's cathedral, and, to those
kneeling before the little altar, they are shown
with prescribed devotion, one by one. A cynic
once wrote, "Faith is the capacity for believing
what we know cannot possibly be true." But
there is not a shadow of doubt on the faces of
those kneeling people seeking relief for spiritual and physical ills. There is said to be a
piece of the staff of Moses; a lock of the hair
with which Mary Magdalene wiped the feet of
Christ; the sandals of Saint Peter; crumbs left
from the feeding of the Five Thousand; one of
the thirty pieces for which Judas betrayed his
Lord; the swaddling clothes of Christ; his
shroud; thorns from his crown; part of the

344

Cross upon which he died; the rod which the Jews mockingly placed in his hands; a bit of the earth upon which last he stood; and the Cruz de la Victoria, always carried by Pelayo in the Covadonga victories.

Covadonga, only a few mountain miles from Oviedo, will forever remain sacred in the annals of Spain, for here, in the crowning of Pelayo, whose romantic life has been embroidered with many a legend, was reborn the native dynasty. According to fable, Pelayo's mother was Doña Luiz, sister of Roderick of Toledo fame, and passionately loved by the reigning king. But a certain Favila, lord of the iron-bound coast of Asturias, also loved her and, with the consent of Doña Luiz, went through a secret simplified form of marriage in the lady's bedroom, before a statue of the Virgin. In course of time, Doña Luiz became a mother and fearing the anger of the King, she placed her son upon a raft, setting it adrift on the river Tagus. As it floated away, a radiant light appeared about the sleeping child, who was later to become the savior of his country in driving out the Moors.

After the disastrous battle of Guadalete, in which Roderick lost his throne and his life,

345

Pelayo with three hundred followers took refuge in the ancestral home of his father. For years he carried on the same sort of guerrilla warfare that played so important a part, centuries later, in the Carlist conflicts.

Pelayo's stronghold was the rock of Covadonga, an ideal natural citadel, whose steep wooded slopes are battlemented by a fringe of sharp peaks, with a glimpse beyond of pathless pines and farther higher summits wreathed in snow. Full in the face of the rock is the mouth of a deep cave, a narrow way leading to it ending there, Nature forbidding further progress. Here it was that the little band of Gothic chieftains, dressed in jerkins of homespun, gathered together. Fleeing representatives of a nation conquered and seemingly helpless, they chose as their leader that Pelayo who, by invincible courage and wisdom, had saved them time and time again from total extinction. Upon his head they placed an iron crown, hastily formed from the points of Moorish spears taken from enemy foes. They bound together their shields into a rude litter upon which they bore their chief back and forth before the entrance of the cave with exultant shouts, their heads bared and their naked swords held aloft.

COVADONGA, OVIEDO.

Now began the reconquest of Spain. Pelayo and his dauntless followers, prepared to fight to the death, made a stand against the Moorish hordes sent to ferret them from out their hiding place. Within this veritable cul-de-sac at the head of Covadonga Valley, the Goths awaited their foes, who, trusting to numerical strength, blindly pushed ahead through the intricate recesses of the mountain. But disordered by the steep, broken ground and exposed to the avalanche of rocks that were hurled from above, the Moors were overwhelmingly routed.

Today an obelisk marks the spot where Pelayo was crowned king, and upon the summit of the rock stands the church dedicated to the Virgin of Covadonga, Our Lady who from heaven fought so valiantly as to bring this miracle victory to the Goths, who were only three hundred against thirty thousand.

The beetling precipice overhanging the famous cave is now fringed with ivy and drooping fern, while a wooden balcony leads to a rock-hewn sepulcher containing the body of Pelayo and also to a rather tawdry chapel for his adoring worshipers. Covadonga has long been a national cult, a place of pilgrimage, whose always overcrowded primitive hotels are probably one

347

form of penance. But this romantic spot is so glorified by nature, screened, as it is, by a dark chain of mountains over which rear those grandiose Picos de Europa, the landmark of old navigators steering their argosies, that all discomfort is forgotten.

One should visit Covadonga in September, when the peasantry, wearing penitent robes, bring offerings in fulfillment of some vow. Mass is said in the open air, and the sermon is preached from a pulpit hung from a great tree. Afterwards, in procession, around and around this natural auditorium is carried the Virgin, trailed by the pilgrims holding lighted tapers.

A few kilometers through savage defiles and the sea bursts upon us in all its sun-dazzling glory, singing a color song in the key of blue, with modulations, in answer to the fleeting movements of the clouds. In magic change the sea fuses with the sky, so that its ships are floating in a silver haze of cloud, their sails splendid with light—a light drenching the mountain side that in places leans with rugged elbow far over the waters. The beauty of this way along the sea is unsurpassed. We linger so often beside sandy beaches offering some glorious distant view of cliff and headland that before we realize it Helios dives into the ocean, kissing the blue with rosy lips, and a flood of color breaks in billows of fire over the ragged sky line. As he disappears in glory, an old woman, bronzed and still vigorous, with the bold eyes of Asturia, bows her head and kneels before the wayside cross. It is the hour of *Ave.*

Shielded by a rocky screen, beautiful Santander lazily suns herself on the doorstep of the ocean, awaiting her lord and master, the King, whose summer palace stands on the far end of one of the green spurs that jut far out into the blue water, giving unimpeded view of the charming bay and the snow-capped heights of the higher mountains. The King will arrive in the gay sunshine of a Spanish August, when Santander dons her fashionable attire and the handsome villas that dot the coast will be bright with aristocratic life.

Always close to the sea we ride until nearing Bilbao, that wide-awake, prosperous city, seething with industrialism—and incidentally with anarchism. The river harbor is a thick forest of steamer funnels, the streets black with people, over whom hangs a continuous bronze haze from the smoke of the blast furnaces to which she owes her blatant prosperity.

We hasten through the un-Spanish city, stopping only at the Misericordia, whose sainted sisters, here, as elsewhere in Spain, mother abandoned children. One of the stone walls of this convent is windowless, but there is a large square panel of wooden planking, tightly closed, with an electric push button plainly showing to the right. Presently we see a slim, girlish figure, cloaked by the shadows of night, furtively steal toward this pious refuge, clasping a love child close to her breast. Quivering with anguish, her hand seeks the bell. At length the trembling fingers find it, and they give a timorous push. A moment of agonized waiting, and the panel slowly drops to right angles with the wall, bringing up, as it falls, another panel that closes the opening so that no one can see from within. On the now projecting platform, swung from rigid iron supports, is a tiny cradle. Looking about, nervously, the girl thrusts her sleeping baby into the cradle nest, kneeling for a moment by its side for one long last kiss. A convulsive sob, and again she rings the bell,—and withdraws into the shadows. The panel moves slowly upward, gradually shutting the child from sight, and the girl disappears into the night—alone.

Again the sea, its shore a diadem of villages set in yellow sand. To the deep tint of the sky the ocean answers with a vivid blue, bathing the earth in profound quiet and peace; the only echo of the world's storms is the beating of surf against the rocks below.

It scarcely needs the frequent coats of arms, proudly blazoned on the broad-eaved farm-house, to tell us we are back again in the country of the superstitious Basques. Only here could be seen that loosened roof tile, pushed aside so that it leaves a hole into the room below. Some one of the inmates has just died and the opening in the roof has been made that his soul may with ease fly to heaven.

Once again San Sebastián, and once again we cross the bridge over the river Bidassoa, stirring into temporary life the somnolent customs officials. Yes, we are a bit sad that journey's end has come, but our eyes and minds—and our hearts, too—are full of the things they have seen, with memories that are a possession for life.

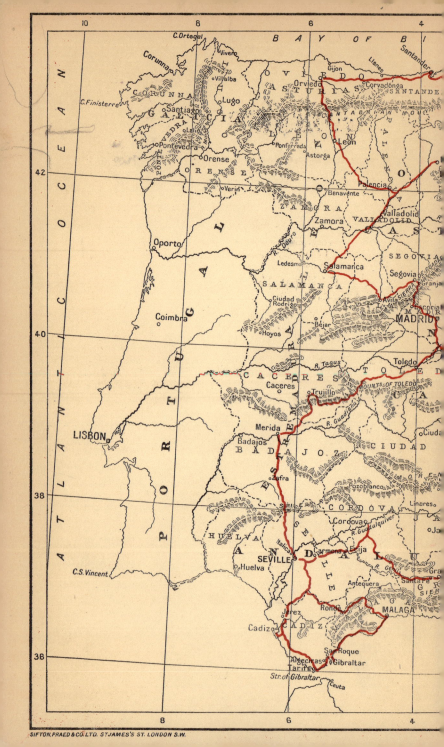